HANDBOOK
OF
VISUAL PERCEPTUAL TRAINING

HANDBOOK
OF
VISUAL PERCEPTUAL TRAINING

By

SUSANNE A. CUNNINGHAM, M.A.

Speech and Language Specialist
Anaheim City School District
Anaheim, California

and

CORA LEE REAGAN, M.A.

Director, Kenwood School
of Special Education
Anaheim, California
Director, Radcliffe Hall
Private School
Anaheim, California

CHARLES C THOMAS · PUBLISHER
Springfield · Illinois · U.S.A.

Published and Distributed Throughout the World by
CHARLES C THOMAS • PUBLISHER
BANNERSTONE HOUSE
301-327 East Lawrence Avenue, Springfield, Illinois, U.S.A.
NATCHEZ PLANTATION HOUSE
735 North Atlantic Boulevard, Fort Lauderdale, Florida, U.S.A.

© *1972, by* CHARLES C THOMAS • PUBLISHER

ISBN 0-398-02267-4

Library of Congress Catalog Card Number 70-165882

With THOMAS BOOKS *careful attention is given to all details of
manufacturing and design. It is the Publisher's desire to present books
that are satisfactory as to their physical qualities and artistic possibil-
ities and appropriate for their particular use.* THOMAS BOOKS *will
be true to those laws of quality that assure a good name and good will.*

Printed in the United States of America
N-1

For the love of all children
who need special help
this book is dedicated.

CONTENTS

HANDBOOK
OF
VISUAL PERCEPTUAL TRAINING

Chapter One

INTRODUCTION

"But, Johnnie, that's a *d* instead of a *b*."

"Susie, the word is *saw* not *was*."

"This is the left side of our paper. Let's all follow this line from left to right."

"Mary, that's the right-hand side. Now, move your hand to the opposite side. That's better. This side is right, and this side is left."

THERE ARE many children to be found in our midst, children who are struggling, or will be struggling, with formal education. Those of you who are in the teaching field have found these children in your classrooms.

Such children may have been diagnosed as unwilling to perform, immature, dyslexic, having learning disorders, mentally retarded, all of these or combinations of these. Frustration is piled upon frustration. Child, parent and teacher become impatient with the child's apparent lack of ability to perform. The tide of emotions runs high!

How can these debilitating emotions be prevented or decreased? What is the role of the parent in helping to prevent or minimize these emotional upsets? What can the child do to help himself? How can the teacher be of help?

After several years of research into the matter, and considerable teaching and training of children found unable to perform satisfactorily in the classroom, some answers to these questions and suggestions for their practical application have been formulated and can be found in the following pages.

It is important to recognize, when children are very young, that their development is other than normal. One purpose of this publication is to assist in the early identification of children who show a delay in refinement of performance of eye and motor control activities.

A second goal is to alert those working with children that deviation from normal eye and motor control development may be indicative of visual perceptual dysfunction. Means of assessing visual perceptual function are then explored.

A suggested guide for programming activities, designed to help in the alleviation of this particular learning disorder, is presented. These activities are planned sequentially and involve visual perceptual and visual-motor performance. The program has been planned to meet specific goals and may be used on an individual or group basis.

Lastly, some suggestions for practical application of the visual-motor perceptual activities in the regular classroom with retarded children, with educationally handicapped and with aphasic children are included.

DEFINITIONS

The following definitions, it is felt, will be helpful in understanding this handbook.

Perception

"Perception is the over-all activity of the organism that immediately follows or accompanies energistic impingements upon the sense organ" (Bartley, 1958). "Hence, in studying perception, we are studying what it is that the organism experiences; not what the physical world contains or is made up of" (Bartley, 1958).

Visual Perception

Visual perception, as used herein, is that process by which impressions observed through the medium of the eye are transmitted to the brain where relationship to past experiences takes place.

Visual Experience

A visual experience can be divided into (a) acuity, (b) recognition, (c) image retention, (d) association with previous visual experience, (e) association with activity symbols and (f) formation of concepts.

Visual perception refers to (b) recognition, (c) image retention, and (d) association with previous visual experience.

Language

Language is the ability to use symbolic expression for purpose of communication. Symbolic expression includes gesturing, speaking, reading, writing and listening. Language becomes useful when the end result is gesturing, speaking, reading, writing and listening.

Speech

Speech is one of the symbolic expressions of language. The speech act is dependent upon auditory perception, articulation and voice. Speech becomes a means of communication when there is understanding of the oral and written word.

Language Disorder

Language disorder is defined as the lack of ability to use symbolic expression for purpose of communication. The term may include disorders of reading, writing, speaking and listening.

Visual Perceptual Deficits as a Syndrome

It is concluded that visual perceptual deficits fall into patterns of a syndrome and that each component may impinge upon any number of other factors or may function independently. Visual perceptual dysfunction does not include lack of adequate visual perceptual stimulation; it does involve improper choice of ontogenetic sequencing for such stimulation. It is not a matter of either-or; rather it is a matter of degree. It represents an inefficient developmental functioning that is a handicap to cognitive process. It is related to both cognition and emotional development.

Concomitant factors of visual perceptual dysfunction may be short attention span, hyperactivity, distractibility, social adjustment difficulties, delayed motor perceptual ability, depressed academic achievement, inadequate body image and low frustration level.

THE RELATIONSHIP OF VISUAL PERCEPTION TO THE PROCESS OF LEARNING

Adequate perceptual functioning is dependent upon previous experiences of both a sensory and a motor nature. Authorities agree that inadequate sensory experiences contribute to perceptual deprivation and influence speech and language development (Myklebust and Johnson, 1962).

Manifestations of this inadequate sensory experience or visual perceptual dysfunction may contribute to the delay of speech and language development in the preschool child. Some characteristics which may accompany delayed perceptual functioning are distractibility, hyperactivity, short attention span, delayed motor perceptual ability, social adjustment disability, inadequate body image and low frustration level.

If a problem of visual perceptual dysfunction is detected in the very young child, the proper training is initiated, there is more likelihood that the child will perform to capacity. "Contact with a rich sensory environment is necessary in childhood to develop an adequate internal model of the external world" (Schultz, 1965). However, when a child reaches the school age, this problem can adversely affect learning and thus constitute a learning disorder. Goins (1958) states that there exists "a general power of visual perception related to reading." Further extension of the relationship to visual perceptual disability and academic achievement would include writing, spelling and tasks involving numbers.

RELATIONSHIP OF SPEED OF PERCEPTION TO PERFORMANCE

It is important to understand that lack of adequate visual perceptual functioning affects the child's rate of performance. Thus, when a child transposes letters, transposes words, or reverses letters, he learns reading, writing, arithmetic and spelling at a slower rate.

There is agreement that motor factors are important in movement of the body in space and impinge upon visual perceptual functioning (Kephart, 1960). The child may appear to be aware of the requirements for performing a task. For instance, in reaching for a balloon a child may reach too far to the right to make contact with the balloon. The child with a visual perceptual handicap may require excessive training in the performance of this act.

Another indication of the interrelatedness of speed of perception and performance is that a child may appear to perceive a whole by parts and be unable to organize these parts into a whole. Strauss and Lehtinen (1947) state that "one basic characteristic of perceiving is that a perception is made of a whole, that it occurs immediately and unanalytically, all at once and nothing first." In a future chapter, a situation is proposed for determining speed of performance. It is felt that some factors influencing the speed of perception are inability to attend, distractibility, hyperactivity, hyperkinesthesia, inconsistency of performance, frustration and short attention span.

There are various types of perceivers: those who, for instance, scan a page several times before beginning performance; those who show a problem in determining a starting point of a given task; and those who show the perseverative behavior. Many children who fall into these classifications of perceivers may be observed to perceive at a reduced rate and to perform at a slower rate than those children who do not fall into these categories.

POSSIBLE EFFECT OF VISUAL PERCEPTUAL DYSFUNCTION ON BEHAVIORAL PATTERNS

It is deemed necessary to mention that, as with most components of learning disorders, emotional overlay may accompany visual perceptual dysfunction. Such emotional overlay may be manifested in guilt, anxiety or hostility or combinations of any of these. There may be interference with normal development of the child's self-concept and, therefore, the child's behavioral patterns may be adversely affected.

IDENTIFICATION OF VISUAL PERCEPTUAL DYSFUNCTION AT THE PRESCHOOL LEVEL

The onus of early identification of visual perceptual dysfunction falls upon either parents or preschool teachers and administrators or upon all of these.

Detection of visual perceptual and/or motor perceptual malfunction at an early age is of prime importance. Some general areas to be observed are as follows:

Delay in gross muscle development (e.g. general clumsiness, falling often, inability to pick up large blocks and place them in a specific place).

Delay in fine muscle development (e.g. inability to stay within the lines when coloring a large picture).

Delay in ability to judge position of an object (e.g. in attempting to grasp an object suspended in space, may misjudge position of object).

The Growth Patterns in Chapter 5 may be consulted for indications of visual perceptual dysfunction at the preschool level.

IDENTIFICATION OF VISUAL PERCEPTUAL DYSFUNCTION IN THE CLASSROOM

How does the classroom teacher discover dysfunction of visual perception? Teacher identification of visual perceptual deficiencies may include rating of classroom performance and motoric behavior.

Some clues to malfunction in general areas of development which may possibly be a part of the syndrome of visual perceptual dysfunction are as follows:

Delay in reading ability.

Delay in ability to use crayon or pencil (e.g. inability to trace lines and to color within lines).

Delay in motor perceptual abilities (e.g. inability to catch a ball; inability to walk a straight line).

In the Appendix, Table II is a teacher rating scale. This form is a working tool for the classroom teacher in determining the frequency and severity of the concomitant factors relating to lack of ability to visually perceive adequately.

SUGGESTED AREAS TO BE EMPHASIZED IN A TRAINING PROGRAM

It is felt that, in order to alleviate the manifested visual perceptual problems, an integrated program involving speech and language activities, a wide range of sensory modalities and visual-motor perceptual activities would be beneficial.

Authorities recommend the inclusion of various experiences in visual perceptual training. Frostig (1965) discusses a multidisciplinary approach to the problem of visual perceptual functioning with emphasis on motivation. This authority also recommends a program built upon previous experiences that moves from gross to fine motor activities. Development of specific methods for visual motor and visual perceptual training should include motor rhythm activities, body image training, spatial and directional relationships and should be built upon previous successes and move from concrete to abstract, Strauss and Lehtinen (1947).

All of the aforementioned areas of specific training are included in the recommended training program (Chap. 6).

SUMMARY

Visual perception, as used herein, is that process by which impressions observed through the medium of the eye are transmitted to the brain where relationship to past experiences takes place. This process is imperfect in many children of various ages. These children may be unable to perform, in one or more areas, at the level of most children of the same age. Terms such as *unwillingness to perform, immaturity* or *mentally retarded* (all of these or any combination) may have been used in describing those youngsters, while, in reality, inability to adequately perceive visual stimuli may be a part of the problem.

Visual perception is closely related to the process of learning. Adequate motor perception is viewed as antecedent to visual perception and is, therefore, an important process in cognition. Speed of perception, both visual and motor, may be found to be related to classroom performance.

Those children who show a deficiency in the visual perceptual process may also have emotional problems. Emotional overlay may develop as the result of successive failures. Therefore, early, precise identification of visual perceptual dysfunction is imperative if a child is to function adequately in a school setting. Once identification of visual perceptual dysfunction as a part of a syndrome has been made, training of various, specific aspects is indicated to assure success in school performance.

Chapter Two

PRACTICAL USE OF THE HANDBOOK

T HE *Handbook of Visual Perceptual Training* was written for parents, teachers and all others working with children for two purposes: (a) to assist in early recognition of defective visual perceptual functioning, and (b) to present a training program designed to improve visual perception, and suggestions for implementation of this program.

In order to make practical use of this handbook it will be necessary to determine as definitively as possible which aspect, or aspects, of the act of visually perceiving are defective and, therefore, require training. Some general areas of visual perception (coordination of eye-motor movements, distinguishing foreground from background, visual memory, spatial position and relationship to space) are considered in this book. Also, it will be necessary to know at what level to begin the training. This will insure effective and efficient usage of the proposed training program and accompanying training kit (Chap. 6).

It is recommended that a battery of tests be used for such evaluation if a psychologist and speech therapist are available to administer the instruments. Tests that may be used in this evaluative method are Goodenongh Draw-A-Person Test, Gesell Developmental Schedules, four subtests of the Illinois Test of Psycholinguistic Abilities and the Frostig Developmental Test of Visual Perception. These instruments will be discussed at length in this chapter under "Measurement of Visual Perceptual Functioning."

In cases where services for obtaining results on standardized tests are not available, it is suggested that indication of visual perceptual imperfection be gained by observation and consulting the case history, if available. Also, the Growth Patterns (Chap. 5), may be used to obtain general clues to dysfunction of the act of visually perceiving. The Growth Patterns were designed to be used as a reference to child development. The visual-motor perceptual performance of a specific child may be compared to these schedules.

Once verification of an impairment has been made and the level of functioning has been determined, the training program, as outlined in Chapter 6, and the accompanying training kit may be successfully used. The activities included in the proposed training program were sequentially planned, and guidelines for implementation were set forth.

Visual perceptual dysfunction as it pertains to specific groups, i.e. those children classified as having learning disabilities, aphasia and mental retardation, is discussed in Chapter 3. Some suggestions for working with young-sters in these categories are included in the same chapter.

MEASUREMENT OF VISUAL PERCEPTUAL FUNCTIONING

Teachers in regular classrooms, special education teachers, reading spe-cialists and all others working with children may request assessment by a qualified person if such service is available. A battery of tests may include the following:

1. Goodenough Draw-A-Person Test, Florence L. Goodenough, Ph.D. (1963).
2. Gesell Developmental Schedules, Arnold Gesell and others (1949).
3. Four subtests of the Illinois Test of Psycholinguistic Abilities, Samuel A. Kirk and James J. McCarthy (1968): Subtest #3, Visual Memory; Subtest #6, Visual Association; Subtest #7, Visual Closure and Sub-test #10, Manual Expression.
4. Developmental Test of Visual Perception, Marianne Frostig, Welty Lefever and John R. B. Whittlesey (1966).

A description of these instruments and the reason for their suggested use are given below.

Determining Body Image

To learn the developmental level of body image of a child is important, it is felt, in assessment of visual perceptual functioning. The Draw-A-Person Test, also called the Goodenough Intelligence Test, yields a mental age which establishes the year and month of body image development.

In review of the 1926 edition of the test, Naomi Steward (1953) states: "It compares favorably in test-retest reliability with most group tests of in-telligence applicable in the same group." Steward adds that its demonstrated correlations with the Stanford-Binet, for the age group for which it was designed, compare favorably in validity. The authors view body image de-velopmental age as relating to motor perceptual-cognitive abilities.

Assessment of Ability to Copy Forms

The ability to copy forms, it is postulated, is a correlate of the act of vis-ually perceiving and, subsequently, of the process of learning. Scores indicat-ing the developmental level of this aptitude can be obtained by administer-ing the Gesell Developmental Schedules. The child is required to copy the circle, cross, square, triangle and diamond, and the resulting scores range from three to seven years.

In reviewing the test, Emmy E. Werner (1959) states:

Gesell Developmental Schedules have been used fairly extensively as a criterion measure in the follow-up of infants with complications at birth or as predicators of intellectual development in the preschool and early school years.

Werner also states that members of the medical profession, especially pediatricians and neurologists, are enthusiastic for use of Gesell. The reviewer feels, however, that there is need for restandardization of Gesell Schedules in consideration of changes such as infant behavior, improvement in nutrition and pediatric care, changes in views on rearing children and differences in various socioeconomic and ethnic groups.

Knobloch and Pasamanick (1959) report high correlation between Gesell and three-year-olds and the Stanford Binet and a correlation of .50 between forty-week scores on Gesell and seven-year intelligence test scores.

Evaluation of Psycholinguistic Abilities

The four subtests of the Illinois Test of Psycholinguistic Abilities were included as part of the battery of tests for evaluating visual perceptual ability. Scores obtained on this instrument are interpreted in terms of psycholinguistic age in year and months and a standard score of deviation.

The tasks presented in the Visual Memory subtest of the Illinois Test of Psycholinguistic Abilities (1968) measure the degree to which a subject is able to retain a visual image. Accurate visual memory is an important part of the visual perception process and is considered a key to success in reading as well as other academic subjects.

Visual Association, a subtest of the 1968 edition of the Illinois Test of Psycholinguistic Abilities (ITPA), assesses the ability of the examinee to perceive picture association and to respond by pointing to the selection.

The Visual Closure subtest of the ITPA examines the facility of the child in recognizing a familiar picture and distinguishing it from other pictures.

Manual Expression (1968 version) taps the skill of the subject to communicate by gesture. Performance on this subtest of the ITPA involves motor-perceptual activity and body scheme awareness.

According to McCarthy and Kirk (1963) it is not possible to concisely summate the validity of the ITPA battery and subtests. These authors state that the adequacy of the concurrent, construct and predictive validities is suggested in a general manner by the data.

The ITPA battery was correlated with other tests of a linguistic nature, i.e. reading sections of achievement tests, verbal performance intelligence tests and Peabody Picture Vocabulary Test. Fairly typical concurrent and predictive validity coefficients were found. Varying degrees of concurrent and predictive validity appear on individual ITPA subtests as indicated by McCarthy and Kirk. The subtest, Visual-Motor Association (1961 edition) and Visual Association (1967), was judged to have an excellent degree of concurrent and predictive validity; Visual-Motor Sequencing (1961) or Visual Memory (1968) an intermediate degree and Motor Encoding (1961), renamed Manual Expression in the 1968 edition, a doubtful degree of concurrent and predictive validity, McCarthy and Kirk.

Precise Measurement of Visual Perceptual Ability

In order to obtain precise measurement of certain visual perceptual performance, it is recommended that the Developmental Test of Visual Perception, Marianne Frostig, Welty Lefever and John R. B. Whittlesey (1966) be administered. The five subtests of this instrument are conceived to be important parts of the process of visually perceiving and have particular relevance to school performance. Each of the subtests yields an age eqivalent (perceptual age level) which is calculated in terms of the performance of the average child in that particular age group.

The Developmental Test of Visual Perception was reviewed by James M. Anderson and Mary C. Austin (1965). Anderson reports that "reliability and validity studies are done on inadequate samples of varying age groups." Validity has been investigated through correlation between Scaled Scores and teacher ratings of classroom adjustment, − .44; motor coordination, − .50 and intellectual functioning, − .50. Correlation between Frostig and Goodenough ranges from .32 to .46.

In a study of twenty-five children, the Frostig test proved to be highly accurate in identifying children who would not attempt to learn to read at the time of exposure. Subtest scale scores test-retest correlations are reported to range from .42, Figure-Ground, to .80, Form Constancy, James M. Anderson and Mary C. Austin (1965).

DETECTION OF POSSIBLE VISUAL PERCEPTUAL DYSFUNCTION WITHOUT PROFESSIONAL HELP

If a psychologist, psychometrist or speech therapist is not available for the evaluative service, the Growth Patterns (Chap. 5) may be used to obtain an indication of imperfect visual perception. By using the Growth Pattern for comparison to specific performance of a child, a general idea about the presence and severity of the handicap may be gained.

The case history gives information pertinent to childhood development and may provide answers to some of the examiner's questions. If a child has a history of delayed development in physical coordination, communications skills and social performance, the possibilty of below level of expectancy of visual perceptive abilities becomes greater.

GROWTH PATTERNS

The Growth Patterns (Chap. 5) were developed to be used as a reference in detecting deviation from the typical pattern of child development at specific ages.

Attention at this time is directed to the suggested method for use of the Growth Patterns. The examiner is advised against adhering rigidly to the schedules. Assume that it is discovered that a certain six-year-old child frequently writes the letter *d* when the intention was to make the letter *b*. The examiner may consult the Growth Patterns for five- to six- or six to seven-year olds. In these particular age brackets is an item which indicates that a child falling within these age limits might typically produce a *d* instead of a *b*. Also, the four-year-old, as seen by the four- to five-year performance schedules, may manifest this type of performance.

In a case such as this, it suggested that other areas of development be examined for delay in maturation. This is not conclusive proof of visual perceptual dysfunction. Further examination of awareness of spatial position is warranted. The concept of left to right is involved in the process of distinguishing a *d* from a *b*, and various test of directionality awareness may be devised. For example, the child in question may be asked to choose from a row of four horizontal arrows, the arrow that is pointing in a different direction from the others.

If the subject has difficulty distinguishing a *p* from a *b*, the concept of up and down may not be well established. The child may, in this case, be required to select from a row of four vertical arrows the one that is turned in a different direction from the other arrows.

The purpose of the preceding explanation is to emphasize the fact that there is considerable overlapping of expected performance at various age levels. Significant deviation from typical performance in several areas, as determined by using the Growth Patterns, may indicate visual-motor perceptual dysfunction.

In developing the Growth Patterns, effort was made to include all aspects of child development: physical, speech and language and social performance. In order to facilitate their use, items have been grouped according to the above-listed areas and each has been appropriately captioned.

TRAINING FOR VISUAL PERCEPTUAL DISABILITY

Once visual perceptual dysfunction has been detected and complete assessment of level of performance has been made, an individualized program may be planned. Careful planning is required to adequately meet the needs of the child.

At this point, the proposed training program (Chap. 6) may be used. It is necessary for the trainer to be aware of the various needs of the child: motor, communications, social and emotional. Also it is important that the trainer understand the relationship of these needs one to the other and their attendant effect upon the behavior of the child. The program is designed to assist in this respect.

A Proposed Training Program

The purpose of the proposed training program is to help specialists, teachers or anyone working with the language disorder of visual perceptual dysfunction in preparing activities to improve abilities which are deficient. Suggested activities are grouped under five main headings: coordination of eye-motor movements, distinguishing foreground from background, visual memory, spatial position and relationship to space. Attention is called to the careful ordering of tasks in the outline. For example, a child generally cannot be expected to copy a square until the skill of reproducing a circle has been accomplished. Therefore, in order to avoid possible frustration, the forms should be presented circle first.

Included in the activities of the program are speech, language and visual-motor perceptual tasks that involve use of all senses. Outline form is employed so that purposes and goals can easily be followed.

The program consists of a sequence of specific educational methods within each purpose, and there is much overlapping of objectives. For example, if the objective is to improve ability to distinguish foreground from background, the learning may be simultaneously extended. See the procedures in Chapter 6 under "Ability to Distinguish Foreground from Background." Improvement can be expected in balance, body image, verbalization, awareness of geometric forms and many other language and motor abilities.

In designing the program, major emphasis was placed on relating all activities, whether motor, kinesthetic, visual or other, to reading, writing and arithmetic.

Training Kit

To facilitate use of the outline described above, a list of aids has been included in Chapter 6 under "Training Kit." The items, when used with the program, stimulate the various senses. All listed items are readily available commercially or can easily be constructed. One item may be employed in accomplishing several goals.

VISUAL PERCEPTUAL DYSFUNCTION AS IT PERTAINS TO SPECIFIC GROUPS OF CHILDREN

For those working with children placed in classified groups, such as learning disorders, aphasia and mental retardation, some specific considerations are given in Chapter 3. These suggestions will prove valuable to successful use of the training program.

SUMMARY

The purpose of this chapter is to give suggestions for the practical use of the handbook. Of first concern is the establishment of the fact that there does exist a deficit in visual perceptual performance. Some standardized measurements of this act of perceiving are Goodenough Draw-A-Person, Gesell Developmental Schedules, certain subtests of the Illinois Test of Psycholinguistic Abilities and the Developmental Test of Visual Perception. It is recommended that a qualified person administer these instruments.

If such assessment is not available, the Growth Patterns in Chapter 5 may be consulted for comparing the performance of a child with that of a typical child from two to twelve years of age. The developmental schedules are arranged under the headings of physical development, speech and language development and social development.

Those working with children are cautioned to be aware of the individual differences in level of development of children.

Visual perceptual dysfunction, according to the authors, is to be classified as a learning disability and language disorder. Detection of the presence and degree of visual perceptual dysfunction as manifested by children with learning disorders and the relationship of this disorder to the process of learning are discussed.

The list of possible concomitant factors of visual perceptual dysfunction may be lengthy.

Imperfect visual perception may also be a learning disorder in aphasia and mental retardation. This handbook can be used in training children placed in these categories as well as with all other children with such handicap.

Chapter Three

LEARNING AND VISUAL PERCEPTUAL FUNCTIONING

L EARNING is the process of acquiring skill or habit or modifying existing habit or skill by means of experience, practice or exercise. This experience, practice or exercise may be gained in an instructional setting or, without the assistance of an instructor, simply by trial and error.

Learning gained through the visual perceptual mode includes recognition, image retention and association with previous visual experience.

The child with a visual perceptual deficit may perceive a visual image but not recognize it; may recognize the image but not retain it; may perceive, recognize and retain the image but may lack the ability to associate this image with past visual experience.

The term *learning disability* refers to any factor which inhibits, or alters, this process of acquiring skill or habit through experience, practice or exercise.

The purpose of this chapter is to discuss visual perceptual functioning as it relates to learning and to classify the deficiency as a learning disorder, or disability.

VISUAL PERCEPTUAL DYSFUNCTION AS A LEARNING DISABILITY

Visual perceptual dysfunction, according to the authors, is to be classified as a learning disability or disorder. It must be remembered that visual perceptual deficits fall into patterns of a syndrome and that each component may impinge upon any number of other factors or may act independently. To reiterate, concomitant factors of visual imperfection may be short attention span, hyperactivity, distractibility, disorganization, apprehension, social adjustment difficulties, delayed motor perceptual ability, depressed academic achievement, hostility, low frustration level and compulsive behavior.

If a child is unable to perceive objects, or words, through the eye in a normal manner, the process of learning is likely to be impaired in some way. The concern, for those working with children, is not so much with the absence or presence of visual perceptual handicap but with the degree of such disability.

VISUAL PERCEPTUAL DYSFUNCTION IN SPECIFIC GROUPS

The authors like to refrain from placing labels on children who, for any number of reasons, fail to be as proficient in performance as normally expected of children at that age. However, in order to present the training program so that it will be most meaningful for use with specific groups, some general terms or classifications are used. In describing three general groups of children working below the expected level of performance the terminology employed is *learning disabilities, aphasia* and *mental retardation.*

Visual Perceptual Dysfunction in Learning Disabilities

The term *children with learning disabilities* as used herein refers to children at preschool age or in the regular classroom who are performing below the expected level. It is, however, important to remember that these children may be functioning below the expected level in one or more areas and, at the same time, above in one or more areas. For instance, a child may be working at grade level in arithmetic but reading below grade level.

Learning disabilities may include impairment in hearing or visual acuity, emotional instability, low intelligence, speech problems, language disorders and perceptual handicaps. Consideration is here given to the visual perceptual aspect of learning, and the manner in which it impairs learning is discussed.

Some children, who have met with successive failure in a school setting, may have grown quiet and withdrawn and, consequently, have gone unnoticed. As misbehavior has not developed, the need for testing of a special nature has not been seen. It is not uncommon to find these children passed from one grade to another each year because no management problem has arisen. One or more, or all, of the following may have become a part of the behavioral pattern of such children: cries easily; easily frustrated; does not make friends readily; does not enter into classroom, playground or social activities; is slow in completing a task; is inconsistent in performance; is apprehensive; is unable to remain at one task for a long period of time or perseverates (when required to move from one task to another, the first task is repeated before the new task can be approached). These children may also be handicapped by visual perceptual imperfection.

Children who manifest this learning disorder may be placed in the acting-out group. These children may show some of the above-mentioned behavioral patterns and, also, one or more of the following: hyperactivity; distractibility; keeps others from paying attention; is subject to uncontrolled outbursts for no apparent reason; engages in unacceptable behavior; is hostile, aggressive and has a negative attitude. These children may, or may not, have been tested by a specially trained person.

How does the inability to accurately perceive, through the medium of the eye, become a deterrent to the process of learning? If a child is unable to precisely recognize a visual image, a handicap exists. If the object, or picture, is recognized but not retained or perhaps is kept for only a short period of time, then this constitutes a learning disorder. If the image is recognized and retained, but the child is incapable of forming associations with previous experience, this, too, inhibits learning.

There are children who can recognize, retain and make associations with past visual stimuli, but are not capable of transferring learned information into speech or writing. This is a very brief explanation of the cause for delayed learning.

Along with the physiological aspect of the impedance, the appearance of various destructive behaviorisms is likely to take place. It is often difficult to determine the degree of adverse effect of the one upon the other. It is found, however, that visual perceptual dysfunction is frequently a part of the handicap of children classified as having learning disabilities.

Visual Perceptual Dysfunction in Aphasia

Aphasia is a "loss or impairment of language due to some type of brain injury" (Agranowitz and McKeown, 1964).

Unless the aphasic child is severely handicapped, it may be difficult to detect this condition or to distinguish it from other disorders of speech and language. However, it is not as important that a teacher or parent be able to recognize aphasia as it is imperative to realize that there is a deviation from speech and language performance of the typical child.

As this child is observed in the classroom or at the preschool level, one or more of the following behavioral characteristics may be apparent: he is hyperactive; he has a short attention span; he is easily distracted; he has social adjustment difficulties; he shows delay in visual, auditory and/or motor perceptual ability; he is working below grade level; he is easily frustrated; he is inconsistent in performance; he is apprehensive, hostile, aggressive; he is subject to uncontrolled outbursts; he perseverates; he is unable to remain at a task for a long period of time; he is unable to organize a task. These concomitant factors were listed in the general category of learning disabilities or disorders. Children other than those with aphasia may show these symptoms.

The speech and language dysfunction of an aphasic child may fall on one of numerous points (in terms of degree) between minimal and severe. In severe cases of aphasia there may be a complete absence of speech. Some less severe handicaps of speech and language may appear in the following ways: defective articulation; searching for words (unable to call the name of a common object); misnaming (uses an associated word for a common object, e.g. bounce for ball); transposes letters in words (tar for rat); transposes words in sentences; uses telegraphic speech (omits connectives, prepositions, etc.); perseverates; may use echolalic speech (repeats what others have said) until able to grasp the meaning; may use a jargon word in an otherwise clear statement ("I plomb my ball" for "I bounce my ball"); lacks natural rhythm of speech; shows general language disorganization. The aphasic child is often better able to communicate by means of gesture than by means of verbalization.

The aphasic child is often found to have perceptual handicaps, auditory as well as visual and motor. Visual perceptual impairment may appear in one, or many, ways. For performance of the typical child, consult the Growth Patterns (Chap. 5) and compare the perceptual behavior of a specific child with the developmental schedules.

The child who falls into this category needs special training by a speech and language therapist. Training for this child, as with all other children, should begin at a level to insure success and then become increasingly more difficult. Frequent reassessment and parent counseling are imperative.

Following are some suggestions which may be helpful for those working with the aphasic child. These suggestions may be applicable to all children with language handicaps as well as the aphasic child.

1. Complete assessment and frequent reassessment during training are important.
2. Avoid overstimulation. Structure the program well and limit use of visual and auditory stimulation. Too many bright colors or an excessive number of pictures on the walls, for example, may cause overexcitement.
3. Decrease apprehension. For example, if the child is to go on an outing, inform him of this just prior to departing.
4. In presenting a task, remove all extraneous materials.
5. Present tasks slowly, making certain that the concept is grasped before moving on to another activity.
6. Present, whenever possible, concrete concepts rather than presenting in abstraction.
7. Present materials in sequential order.
8. Gear training to immediate needs and past experiences of the child.
9. Use music and rhythm activities frequently.
10. Use, simultaneously, as many modes as possible, e.g. visual, auditory, tactile. It may be necessary, however, to use them one at a time.
11. Train child individually if necessary.
12. Present a task as many times as necessary.
13. Present tasks in small increments so that child can succeed.
14. Prevent frustration, whenever possible, instead of attempting to cure. For example, when the child begins to show frustration, change the approach, the structure of the situation or the instructional materials before the child becomes unable to perform.
15. Parent counseling is important.

A word of caution to the person working with the aphasic child: inconsistency of performance, low frustration level and defeatist attitude are likely to be manifested.

Visual Perceptual Dysfunction in Mental Retardation

Mental retardation refers to a condition of below average general mental functioning which had its beginning in the developmental period. Impairment in ability to adapt to society is a part of this condition.

It is generally agreed by authorities that the mentally retarded are delayed in speech and language development. As in other classifications involving deviancy of speech and language functioning, the abilities of the mentally retarded may range from total absence of speech and severe language deficits to the ability to use and communicate ideas at a subaverage level. This communication includes speaking, listening, reading, writing, arithmetic and spelling.

As the mental retardate is viewed in the classroom or at the preschool level, one or more of the following may be apparent: generally immature behavior; short attention span; distractibility; delayed auditory, visual and motor perceptual ability; depressed academic achievement; inadequate body image; inability to remain at a task for a long period of time or to organize a task; difficulty learning by concept; does not exceed the expectancy level in any academic area; demonstrates below average intellectual functioning in all modes of learning. It will be remembered that some of these characteristics were listed as concomitant factors in the general category of learning disorders and also in the aphasic child. Mentally retarded children may show the same types of speech and language disorders as listed in other classifications; however, they may be more numerous and of a more severe nature.

Deviancy from typical speech and language abilities may appear in defective articulation, omission of speech sounds, omission of words in sentences, shorter sentence length, limited vocabulary, voice problems, dysfluency, lack of natural rhythm in speech and greater ability to gesture rather than to verbalize.

Some suggestions which may be helpful for those who work with these children are as follows:

1. Complete assessment and frequent reassessment are important.
2. Child learns well through drill.
3. Present less material and at a slower rate.
4. Present learning in conceptual form if possible.
5. Present concrete concepts rather than presenting in abstraction.
6. Structure each learning situation.
7. Use music and rhythm activities frequently.

8. Gear all training to the child's immediate, individual needs and experiences.
9. Present materials in sequential order (see Chap. 6 for suggested training program).
10. Design program to include speech, listening and associating activities.
11. Plan to use, simultaneously, as many modes as it is possible to use, e.g. visual, auditory, tactile and kinesthetic.
12. Train child individually if necessary.
13. Present task as many times as necessary for child to succeed.
14. Prevent frustration, whenever possible, instead of attempting to cure. When the child begins to show frustration, change the approach, the structure of the situation or the aids used before the child becomes unable to perform.
15. Parent counseling is important.

SUMMARY

As visual perceptual dysfunction is likely to impair the process of learning, it is to be considered a learning disability or disorder. In this handbook, the authors have often stated that it is important to know the manner in which the learning of a specific child is adversely affected by this handicap. Does the child perceive, recognize and retain a visual image? Is the child able to associate the visual image with past experiences of a visual nature? The trainer will want the answers to these and other questions.

This learning disability is most likely to be found in children working below grade level. These children may have been classified under one of three general descriptive terms: learning disabilities, mentally retarded or aphasic. Some specific suggestions for those working with subjects thus categorized follow descriptions of these terms. It is to be noted that the visual perceptual problems may appear in the same manner in children under various specific groups. The presented suggestions, if followed, will insure a higher level of confidence for success in the use of the training program and instructional aids.

Chapter Four

GENERAL CONSIDERATIONS

In THIS CHAPTER some basic general considerations important to successful training of the child with visual perceptual dysfunction are discussed. These aspects are applicable in all teaching or training of children.

It is imperative that the trainer recognize the talents of each child and maintain an awareness of individual differences of performance among children. Also, it should be kept in mind that emotional overlay may adversely affect one or all of the sensory modalities.

Keeping an open line of communications at all times among those involved with a specific child is of prime importance.

Statistical results of research into visual perceptual deficits of children with learning disorders are reported. Also, the results and observations made during the study and the relationship of these findings to authoritative conclusions are discussed.

INDIVIDUAL DIFFERENCES

It is important, first, to view the subject as a child, to consider him as such and then approach the task at hand, whether it be observing, evaluating or training.

Also, it is imperative that the trainer be aware, at all times, of individual differences in level of development in all areas. Included in these developmental areas are the physical, emotional, social, speech and language aspects. As developmental levels of each child are likely to vary, the needs of each child, physical, emotional, social and communications needs, may differ. For example, one child six years of age may require a longer period of conditioning than another six-year-old or less time at a given task.

As a result of these differences, not every child can be managed in the same manner, nor can the same program of training be presented at the same time and at the same rate of speed.

The Growth Patterns which appear in Chapter 5 will assist the examiner in approximations of differences in level of performance. Rate of performance and effective methods of presentation may be gained by observation of or working with a child.

COMMUNICATION

The importance of communication cannot be overemphasized. Continual feedback from each person, involved in working with a specific child, to all others interested in this subject is of prime importance. Parents, physicians, nurses, psychologists, speech and language specialists, social workers, physical therapists, occupational therapists and other persons in contact with the child are encouraged to communicate frequently.

MOTIVATION AND STIMULATION

To view the subject as a child first has been emphasized. Subsequently, it is important to see the child as an individual and to look for and recognize the talent, or talents, of that individual. Every youngster is able to perform better in one area than in other areas and also to respond more successfully to some methods of presentation of a task than to others.

Beginning training by involving the area, or areas, of strength or talent is more likely to lead to success. At the same time, it is important to base presented tasks on sound educational objectives. The proposed training program (Chap. 6) follows these recommendations.

EMOTIONAL OVERLAY

It should be kept in mind that emotional overlay may adversely affect any one or all of the sensory modalities. In the study cited at a later point in this chapter it was observed by the trainers and verified by teacher evaluation that all twelve subjects of the study manifested emotional instability. Postulation as to why there may be a relationship between perception and emotional stability has been discussed at length in the literature.

One parameter of the correlation of perception and state of emotion is considered at this time. That is, the first step in self-concept development is recognition of oneself as a living organism, awareness that there are boundaries and that this organism has the capacity to function in the world. If there is interference, in the form of sensori-motor dysfunction, with this basic developmental step, the emotional life is likely to be affected. Visual perceptual dysfunction constitutes a deterrent to the development of the organism and, therefore, may affect the state of emotion. As the child begins to compare his abilities with those of his peers the realization that performance is inadequate may take place. From this awareness, negative feelings may begin to influence the original state of affect.

REPORT OF RESEARCH IN VISUAL PERCEPTION

In the aforementioned study, a group of twelve children, ages five through ten, in a private school for children with learning disorders, was described, evaluated, trained with the program as outlined in Chapter 6 and then retested. Each child was given a battery of tests for the purpose of evaluating visual perceptual ability, trained and retested with the same instruments. The tests and methods used are described at length in Chapter 2.

To determine if the children showed significant improvement following training, the Wilcoxon Matched Pairs Signed-ranks was used. This statistical procedure revealed that the test-retest results of Subtest #6 of the Illinois Test of Psycholinguistic Abilities (Motor Encoding) and Subtest #2 of the Frostig Developmental Test of Visual Perception (Figure-Ground) were significant at .01 level. Significant at the .02 level were Subtest #1 of the Frostig Developmental Test of Visual Perception (Eye-Motor Coordination) and Subtest #3 of the Frostig Developmental Test of Visual Perception (Form Constancy). Significant at .05 level were Subtest #9 of the Illinois Test of Psycholinguistic Abilities (Visual-Motor Sequencing) and the Goodenough Draw-A-Person Test.

Some clinical observations, made during the study, are discussed in this chapter.

Correlation of Auditory, Visual and Motor Perceptual Functioning

The investigators agree with Strauss, Lehtinen (1947) and Kephart (1968) that there exists a correlation among auditory, visual and motor perceptual functioning. It is the purpose of the writers, first, to discuss this interrelationship from a clinical viewpoint and, secondly, to report the observed results of the intersensory interaction upon speech, language and academic achievement.

Upon presentation of a task involving any one or all modalities (auditory, visual and motor perceptual) during the use of the training program, the examiner is advised to begin the instructional period with verbal direction. As this first contact normally requires adequate auditory perceptual ability before a child can perform, the subject, of necessity, is required to auditorily perceive the verbal direction.

From observation during the study it was found that the twelve subjects participating in the training program showed varying degrees of ability to follow the verbal cue. Observed results of this ability ranged from total inability to follow the direction to ability to recall only some portion of the verbalization. In some cases only the first part, others only the middle part and still others only the last part of the command was perceived. A further lack of auditory perceptual ability noted was in failure of the subjects to properly sequence activities initiated by verbal direction.

The possibility that subjects might be capable of performing some tasks solely by visual stimulation was taken into consideration in reporting the above observations. It would seem, therefore, that there is a direct relationship between auditory perception and ability to perform. For this reason, an extensive conditioning and auditory training period, as described in Chapter 6, is recommended.

In many tasks included in the training program, aids to visual stimulation are to be presented concurrently with auditory direction. It was found, from observation, that the twelve subjects involved in the training program showed varying degrees of ability to follow the visual cue. Some manifested total inability to gain from visual stimuli. Others were unable to perceive the whole of a visual image and/or failed to sequence properly activities involving visual stimulation. Until such time as the direction was visually perceived correctly, the subjects were unable to perform acceptably. In reporting this observation of visual perceptual functioning, the likelihood that some subjects were capable of performing some tasks solely by auditory perception was not overlooked.

In many activities of the proposed training program, physical action of the trainer is to be used, along with auditory and visual cues, in directing the performance. It was observed that the twelve subjects of the study showed varying degrees of ability to duplicate gesture, or movement. As with auditory and visual perceptual ability, a wide range of motor perception was discovered. Some of the subjects were incapable of reproducing viewed movements, could duplicate only a portion of the act and/or failed to sequence properly these movements.

The observations, described above, tend to strengthen the possibility of high correlation among auditory, visual and motor perceptual functioning.

Relationship of Speed of Perception and Performance

The authors agree with Goins (1968) that there exists a close relationship between speed of perception and performance. In the clinical setting, several observations point to this relationship. One of these is that some children, participating in the reported study, appeared to be aware of the requirements for performing a task but were unable to relate these requirements to themselves. Therefore, excessive time was needed to complete the activity. Other indications of this interrelatedness are reported in Chapter 1.

In order to explore further the relationship between speed of perception and performance, a situation was devised for the subjects of the reported study in which performance was timed. No timing is required for the tasks presented in the training program; therefore, it seemed important to set up a timed procedure.

The task selected for this observation involved visual memory. A flash card, on which a geometric shape was drawn, was briefly presented to each of the twelve children. The subject was then to select from a card, on which several shapes including the stimulus picture were drawn, the duplicate of the originally presented picture. Timing was recorded from the moment the shape was in view of the child until the final selection had been made. Time required for selection varied from two seconds to one minute.

Visual Perceptual Performance of Subjects

Subjects of the study were found to have improved significantly in ability to gesture, awareness of body scheme and performance on visual-motor sequencing tasks. Analysis of the statistical data obtained revealed that the subjects showed significant improvement in motor encoding (significant at the .01 level), in body image (significant at the .05 level as shown by the test-retest scores on the Draw-A-Person) and visual-motor sequencing (significant at .05 level on the ITPA).

Discussion of these results has a twofold purpose. The first is to point out the importance of ability to gesture (motor-encoding), body scheme (as tested on the Draw-A-Person test) and visual-motor sequencing as components of language functioning. The second is to consider body scheme and ability to gesture as learned processes, which may be antecedents of visual-motor sequencing, also a learned process.

The child with a learning disorder often exhibits, along with other language deficiencies, a lack of proficiency in the use of gesture. As gesture is one means of expressing ideas, the ability to use this mode of expression meaningfully serves as an enhancement to expressive language and is indicative of adequate body scheme. Therefore, ability to express ideas gesturally is closely related to the developmental level of body image. This precept corroborates the statement of Kephart (1960): "We need the body image in order to start movement."

Many experiences aimed at improving body image are included in the training program presented to the twelve subjects and appearing in Chapter 6, and body image development is secondary to various other major goals as well. Some of these experiences were designed to improve laterality and directionality, motor perception, spatial relationships and position in space awareness as well as body image. That there was significant improvement of the subjects on performance of the Draw-A-Person is verified by statistical analysis and is at the .05 level of significance. These findings also substantiate the premise that body image is a learned process.

In exploration of the relationship of body image to the motor act and to perception, it will be noted in Chapter 2 that the researchers feel the developmental level of body scheme relates to preceptual cognitive-motor disabilities, and that to learn the developmental level of body image of each subject of a study is important. Again quoting from Kephart (1960): "Only through a reliable and consistent body image can the child develop a reliable and consistent point of origin for either perceptions or motor responses."

Visual-motor sequencing is a learning process involving control of the visual field in relationship to the motor function in a sequencing task. Proper training for the act of sequencing consists of activities which are carefully programmed step by step and may begin with use of body motions which originate from body scheme. One antecedent of visual-motor sequencing, it is believed, is gestural sequencing. This is a good starting point for effective clinical training.

As pointed out in a previous paragraph, adequate body image is a sequel to appropriate, effective use of gesture. Therefore, adequate developmental process involved in the act of visual-motor sequencing is believed to be one of adequacy of body image, meaningful use of gesture and visual sequencing.

Improvement in Proficiency of Classroom Performance

The Teacher Rating Scales used in the reported study (Table II of the Appendix) showed that eleven of the twelve subjects improved in classroom performance after presentation of the intensified, individualized training program. Teacher ratings were on visual-motor perceptual abilities as related to basic classroom subjects of reading, spelling, writing and arithmetic.

One item of the Teacher Rating Scale (Table II in the Appendix) is ability to discover and correct own errors. From this study it was found that one of the most effective methods to use in training children who manifest visual perceptual dysfunction is to encourage them to look for, find and correct their mistakes, e.g. reversals and transpositions of letters or numbers. This procedure can be used advantageously in a clinical setting as well as in the classroom.

Another item which might be added to the check-off on the Teacher Rating Scale is ability to perform visual perceptual tasks from taped directions. This type of activity proved highly successful in training the subjects of the study. It is recommended for use in the classroom as well as in therapy sessions.

Other factors included in the teacher evaluations, completed following the training for the research, were various aspects of state of emotion. From these forms, and parent comment, improved emotional stability was noted in the twelve cases. It is felt that classroom proficiency increased as a result of decreased hyperactivity, distractibility and higher level of confidence and frustration.

SUMMARY

Visual perception is a complex process. It, therefore, seems necessary to explore all impingements upon this act. In reporting the results of a study in the field, the researchers include a multiplicity of influencing factors and discuss their relationship to visual perception. These preliminary considerations will prove valuable to insuring success in the use of the program presented in Chapter 6.

Chapter Five

GROWTH PATTERNS

THE GROWTH PATTERNS have been grouped under three headings: Motor Performance, Communication Performance and Social Performance. The steps in development are not necessarily in sequential order.

To facilitate their use and to show more clearly the possible overlapping of performance, the behaviors were developed for the following age groups; two to three, three to four, four to five, five to six, six to seven, seven to eight, eight to nine and preadolescence.

It is suggested that, in establishing the developmental level of a specific child, consideration be given to the degree of success in performing an act. Is the performance consistent or occasional? Is direction required for performance?

TWO TO THREE

Motor Performance

Assists in dressing and undressing.
Gets a drink unassisted.
Cuts with scissors.
Climbs stairs by alternating feet.
Strings beads.
Holds objects without dropping them.
Turns one page at a time.
Imitates clapping and other hand-arm movements.
Begins to use fingers in grasping crayon.
Copies a circle at age three.

Communication Performance

Identifies object by name.
Obeys commands.
Identifies parts of the body.
Uses the prepositions in front of, under, beside.
Identifies objects by use.
Identifies pictures, e.g. show me what swims.
Uses two or more words in a sentence.
Matches object to object.
Follows four directions using a ball: roll, kick, throw, bounce.
Recognizes action in pictures.

Readily mimics words.
Tells name.
Repeats two digits.
Relates own experiences.
Uses nouns, verbs and pronouns in speech.
Names one color.
Enjoys hearing stories about himself.
Likes nursery rhymes.
Uses words and phrases in speech.
Tells sex by three years of age (boy or girl).
Verbalizes and searches for lost toy.

Social Performance

Enjoys hearing stories about himself.
Understands personal identity.
Likes nursery rhymes.
Relates own experiences.
Imitates.
Recognizes image in mirror.
Engages in both solitary and parallel play.
Likes to wash hands.
Recognizes familiar voices.
Responds to different animal sounds.
Distinguishes between names of familiar relatives.

THREE TO FOUR

Motor Performance

Pours from a pitcher.
Walks down stairs one step at a time.
Runs with ease.
Takes pants off.
Stands without effort.
Balances on one foot for a short period of time.
Walks on toes.
Walks a straight line.
Jumps with feet together.
Catches large ball with extended arms.
Rides a tricycle.
Removes shoe laces.
Unbuttons; cannot button easily.
Washes hands without assistance.
Picks up small objects.
Copies a cross and circle at age four.

Communication Performance

Identifies pictures, e.g. which one gives us milk.
Distinguishes likenesses and differences of objects and pictures.
Tells whether boy is brother and girl is sister.
Acts upon verbal direction.
Selects two objects on command.
Follows directions, e.g. crawl in the box, crawl under the box, crawl on
    top of the box.
Repeats a few rhymes or songs.
Draws and names forms which are not distinguishable.
Performs upon request.
Speaks in sentences.
Attention span of seven to eight minutes.

Social Performance

Does small household chores.
Runs some errands.
Engages in both solitary and parallel play.
Begins to take his turn and to share possessions.
Complies with cultural demands.
Performs upon request.
Zips up pants.
Knows to cover mouth when sneezing or coughing.
Relates experiences.
Seeks help.
Flushes toilet after using.
Knows how to use a spoon when eating.
Knows to wash hands.
Expresses concern when others are hurt.

FOUR TO FIVE

Motor Performance

Hops easily on two feet but not on one.
Skips but not rhythmically.
In climbing stairs, uses one foot, then the other.
Stands on one foot.
With arms extended at sides, moves hand to form circle.
Carries a water-filled object without spilling.
Catches a ball by using arms more than hands.
Enjoys stunts, e.g. somersaults, swinging, whirling.
Buttons coat or dress; still unable to tie shoes.
Makes a fist with one or both hands.

Puts together puzzles of large pieces and single objects.

Imitates, e.g. elephant walking, bird flying, rabbit hopping.

Uses thumb and index finger in grasping.

Places finger on nose with eyes closed.

Jumps a stationary rope.

Marches to music.

Communication Performance

Identifies groups of three.

Counts to four.

Names one or more of the primary colors.

Identifies likenesses and differences.

Names the part that is missing from a single object picture, e.g. bird without a wing.

Follows this direction: Make a circle for the head. Put in eyes and mouth. Make a square for a house and put in the window.

Copies a cross, circle and square.

Shows tendency to conceptualize and generalize.

May misarticulate d, t, n, g, k, ng, y.

Reverses letters b, d.

Discriminates prepositions.

Identifies pictures, e.g. which one is milk?

Understands the concept of three (give me three balls).

Makes opposite analogies; brother is a boy, sister is a _____.

Comprehends what do we do with our nose.

Verbally describes items; what is a dress, a shirt?

Tells what a thing is made of.

Identifies penny, nickel, dime and quarter.

Asks for help.

Social Performance

Participates with other children in playing tag, hide and seek, etc.

Performs small household chores.

Runs errands.

Complies with cultural demands.

Knows to zip up pants.

Knows when to cover mouth.

Dresses himself.

Asks questions, perceives.

Knows when to wipe nose.

Knows how to brush teeth.

Knows and can recognize community helpers.

Knows how to use spoon and fork.

Knows when to use please, thank you and excuse me.

Waits his turn.

Listens and follows simple directions.

FIVE TO SIX

Motor Performance

Folds paper to form a rectangle, triangle or square.

Jumps on two feet and skips fairly rhythmically.

Brushes teeth and combs hair.

Balances on tip toes.

Draws distinct shapes with some detail.

Hops on one foot.

Rolls clay into a ball.

Winds string on a peg.

Balances and uses skates.

Marches to music.

Ties a bow.

Copies a circle, square, cross and triangle.

Has good general motor control.

Large muscles more fully developed than small.

Girls usually about one year ahead of boys in physical development.

Periods of slower physical growth.

Likes to use large muscles (run, jump, etc.) .

Easily fatigued and sitting still is an effort.

Communication Performance

Identifies or names four or more colors.

Counts ten objects.

Folds paper to form a rectangle, triangle or square.

Distinguishes left and right in self.

Prints three- and four-letter words.

Uses money to buy at the store.

Identifies penny, nickel, dime and quarter.

Follows three or four commands in sequence.

Recalls three or four visual experiences (perhaps not in sequence) .

Puts objects and pictures into categories.

Briefly describes a picture or an object.

Articulation is good but still may misarticulate a few sounds.

Likely to reverse letters *b, d.*

Likely to be more organized in his work.

Uses the telephone.

Knows name and address.

Responds best to concrete learning.

Enjoys songs, dancing and rhythms.

Discriminates likenesses and differences in objects and pictures.

Makes opposite analogies, e.g. an inch is short, a mile is —————.

Comprehends what do we do with our feet.

Knows what a ball is made of.

Attention span is fairly short.

Social Performance

Brushes teeth and combs hair.

Interested and competent in performing small household chores.

Interested in playing dress up.

Content to go to school.

Communicates freely with classmates and friends.

Prefers associative play.

Takes some responsibility.

Capable of some self-criticism.

Self-sufficiency and sociability are developed to some level.

Needs approval of the home.

Learning to take turns.

Activities have a definite direction.

Interested in small group activities, but interests are still self-centered.

Needs approval for tasks well done.

Needs to have adults listen to him when he is talking and refrain from interruptions or corrections during this time.

Runs errands and does simple tasks.

Eager to learn.

Beginning to be competitive.

Learns best through participating actively.

SIX TO SEVEN

Motor Performance

Climbs a tree, but balances poorly on a fence.

Tosses, bounces and catches the ball.

Crawls over, under and around large items.

Likes to wrestle.

Swings or pulls himself up on a rope.

Runs and jumps.

Cuts, pastes and works with clay.

Pounds nails, but not too adept at hitting them.

Roller skates and swims.

Uses a pencil.
Uses a table knife for spreading.
Balances standing on one leg.
Throws at a specific target.
Jumps rope.
Draws perpendicular lines,
Manipulates the string of a kite in flying it.
Beginning to lose teeth.
Is better able to hold a pencil.
Improved eye-hand coordination.
Tires easily.

Communication Performance

Answers the telephone.
Counts to thirty.
Tells simple stories.
Relates experiences to a group.
May not be ready for formal reading, writing and arithmetic.
Draws pictures which are crude but lifelike.
Dramatically projects his feelings.
Uses symbols in reading, writing and arithmetic.
Places objects in groups of four or five.
Interested in spatial relationships, e.g. home in relationship to school.
Tells left from right in self, not in others.
Spatial concepts are undifferentiated.
Prints simple words.
Uses a pencil.
Sees general configuration of a word but not its detail, e.g. confuses house
    for home.
Likely to reverse letters.
May still show some poor articulation.
Knows combinations of numbers to ten.
Is in a reading readiness stage.

Social Performance

Delights in reading.
Learns to stand up for own rights.
Restless and may have some nervous habits, e.g. scratching, nail biting,
    etc.
May daydream.
Nightmares caused by overstimulation.
Concerned with right and wrong.

Performs best when activities are alternated, active and quiet.

Is likely to be aggressive.

Answers telephone.

Relates experiences to group.

Functions best in a scheduled routine.

Dramatically projects his feelings.

Likely to dawdle.

Likes to create things as a surprise.

Self-centered.

May be able to accept responsibility for his actions.

Interested in spatial relationships, e.g. home in relationship to school.

Uses the table knife for spreading.

SEVEN TO EIGHT

Motor Performance

Uses table knife for cutting.

Combs or brushes hair.

More cautious in physical activities, e.g. climbing trees, etc.

Repeats performance in order to master it.

Uses baseball and bat and may saw wood.

Apt to drop pencil repeatedly when working as grasp is likely to loosen suddenly.

Dresses self, but may dawdle at this task.

Ties shoe laces tightly.

Rides a bicycle.

More proficient in swimming, sliding, skating and skiing.

Interested in placing and manipulating one object inside another.

May still need to use wide lines for writing.

Likes to play with wheeled toys.

Better small muscle development.

May develop poor posture.

May attempt physical activities beyond capabilities.

Balances on tip toes, bending forward from hips up to ten inches.

Traces through two mazes.

Walks a line placing heel of one foot close to toe of other.

Makes four stacks of nine cards each within thirty seconds.

Taps alternately with feet in rhythmical fashion.

Communication Performance

Counts by ones, twos, fives and tens.

Understands one-half and one-third.

Does simple addition problems.

Understands simple, oral reasoning problems.

May misarticulate some speech sounds.

Tells time to quarter hour.

May perseverate (desire to continue an activity in which he is engaged) .

More aware of relative sizes, e.g. human figures as compared to animals.

Reads alone and enjoys it.

Interested in placing and manipulating one object inside another.

In reading, is likely to omit connectives (and, so, etc.) and may substitute words and vowels.

Likely to erase frequently.

Still shows some reversals but is able to recognize them.

May forget a command and will need to be reminded.

Interested in months and passage of time.

Tells left from right in self, not in others.

Interested in more difficult games, such as Monopoly.®

Social Performance

Uses table knife for cutting.

Combs or burshes hair.

Learns to be a good listener.

Still somewhat self-centered.

Becomes a tattletale.

Dresses self, but may dawdle at this task.

Ties shoe laces tightly.

Responds well to performance in an imaginary situation.

Becomes more aware of self in relationship to his environment.

Sits quietly and plans his activities.

Plays fairly well with other children.

Play is more realistic than imaginary.

More introspective and feeling-centered.

Needs more aggressive directed action.

Competitive.

Displays aggressiveness verbally rather than physically.

Manages small allowance.

Often overanxious because of fear that he cannot meet demands of parents and teachers.

Very sensitive to criticism.

Often careless, noisy and argumentative.

Friendly and interested in people.

Is developing modesty.

Wants a best friend.

Beginning of gang desires.

Needs much praise and encouragement from adults.

EIGHT TO NINE

Motor Performance

Interested in speed; engages in rough and tumble games.

Engages in organized sports and will also observe them.

Likes to perform stunts.

Walks a plank.

Fine muscle coordination is refined; performance is smoother, speedier and more assured.

Spaces words in sentences as he writes.

Shows more accurate body proportions in drawings; can draw action pictures and is beginning to draw in perspective.

Crouches on tiptoes, arms extended and eyes closed.

Touches thumb to all fingers of same hand.

Follows four given directions, e.g. open the window.

Taps floor alternately with feet and taps table with corresponding index finger in same rhythm.

Period of slow but steady growth.

May not get enough rest and may become overstimulated.

Eye-hand coordination good.

Eyes ready for near work with less strain.

Thrives on strenuous exercises but needs lots of rest.

Communication Performance

Beginning to consider cause and effect, e.g. what happens to self and why.

Distinguishes fundamental similarities and differences, e.g. boats, baseball, airplanes.

Likes to talk.

Draws conclusions and implications.

Spaces words in sentences as writes.

Shows more accurate body proportions in drawings; draws action pictures and is beginning to draw in perspective.

Enjoys dramatizing.

Needs assistance in organizing thoughts and activities.

Reads alone.

Transposes words in reading but will maintain meaning.

Occasionally reverses letters.

More aware of value of time, past and future.

Tells right from left on others.

Likely to be high geared and expansive.

Likes realistic as well as make believe.

Social Performance

Interested in speed.

Beginning to consider cause and effect, e.g. what happens to self and why.

Broadening scope of interests.

Somewhat more sensitive (feelings more easily hurt).

Expresses amazement and curiosity.

Engages in organized sports and will also observe them.

Performs household tasks.

Bathes self unaided.

Argumentative.

Interested in environment, going places and doing things.

Has strong sense of right and wrong.

Adults may set too high standards.

Beginning to develop sense of humor.

Interest span is long and performs under self-direction.

Interested in gangs or clubs with only same sex.

Resists neatness (if boy); interested in clothes and looking pretty (if girl).

Beginning to be interested in loyalty to country.

Likes to go camping.

Likes to argue over injustice and fairness.

Quarrelsome and rivals siblings.

Performs well with high-interest activities.

Subject to influence of academic achievement or lack of it.

NINE TO TEN

Motor Performance

Traces through a maze with a pencil.

Balances on one foot, other leg bent at knees and eyes closed, for ten seconds.

Cuts out a circle.

Jumps over a rope, two feet high, without losing balance and claps hands three times while doing this.

Taps floor alternately with feet and taps table with both corresponding index fingers in same rhythm.

Analyzes body motion before and during performance.

Uses hands independently.

Releases tension through fine motor activities, picks at things, shuffles feet.

Participates in fairly well-organized group play.

Eyes ready for close work.
Good eye-hand coordination; ready for crafts.
May fatigue easily.
May still be overly clumsy.
Appetite beginning to be enormous.
Cuts well with scissors.

Communication Performance

Traces through a maze with pencil.
Criticizes others as well as self.
Classifies and identifies.
Interested in detail.
Cuts out a circle.
Brags.
Analyzes body motion before and during performance.
Uses pronoun "we" to identify self in classroom group.
Plans day in consideration of time.
Relates to space by going to one place, e.g. library, without going to another.
Typically uses seven or eight words in a sentence.
Uses adverb clauses.
Describes situations in complex sentence form.
Needs much drill and practice.
Not so easily diverted from a given task.
Likely to be self-motivated and usually well organized.

Social Performance

Girls further developed than boys.
Has sense of right and wrong.
Reasonable and dependable.
Adults may expect too much from this age child.
Beginning to question adult authority.
At the hero worship age.
Often critical of adults.
Enjoys talking and discussing things.
May have disagreements with best friends.
Sibling rivalry very intensive.
Beginning to be a perfectionist.
Developing a distinct personality.
More interested in reality.
May lose interest if discouraged or pressured.
Needs reasonable explanations.

Needs frank discussions about physical development and approaching adolescence.

Better able to learn through example than through lecture.

PREADOLESENCE

Motor Performance

Balances for fifteen seconds on tiptoes with eyes closed.
Balances on one foot at a time on tiptoes for ten seconds.
Jumps, clapping hands three times.
Throws a ball at a target eight feet away.
Makes four piles with forty matches in thirty-five seconds.
Uses crayon in each hand and makes dots simultaneously.
Catches a ball with one hand.
Jumps up onto an object about chair height.
Jumps and touches heels with hands simultaneously.
Sews a design on a sewing card.
Opens and closes one hand at a time, as arms are extended, to a specific rhythm.
Delights in physical activity.
Gross motor coordination much more refined.
Vision picture changed; knows vision blurs after considerable reading.
May still be somewhat clumsy.
Has enormous appetite.
May still tire easily.

Communication Performance

Performs visual task and converses simultaneously.
Makes four piles with forty matches in thirty-five seconds.
Organizes his day well as far as time and energy are concerned.
Organizes thinking so that is able to participate in group discussions.
May use pronoun "he" to designate both genders.
Interested in facts.
Uses oral and written language with facility, clarity and forcefulness.
Uses language to solve problems and to participate in a group.
Meaning becomes attached to abstract terms (patriotism, honesty, etc.) .
Understands several synonyms.
Likes to argue a point.
Fluctuates between extremes.
Enjoys setting up verbal challenges.
Apt to use creative imagination in games, etc.
Likes to talk.

Social Performance

Organizes day well as far as time and energy are concerned.

Organizes thinking so that is able to participate in group discussion.

Aware of individual differences.

Enjoys dramatizing life situations.

Rather sure of self.

Likes to talk.

Attention span still short and needs to move about.

Appears to be relaxed and casual, but alert.

Uses language to solve problems and to participate in a group.

Likes to argue.

Fluctuates between extremes.

Releases tension through fine motor activities, picks at things, shuffles feet, etc.

Boys still enjoy boys, and girls enjoy girls.

Enjoys setting up challenging physical and verbal situations.

Physical and psychological transformations taking place.

Fails to relate well to siblings.

Apt to use creative imagination in games, etc.

Highly competitive.

Boys may mature as much as two years later than girls.

Very sensitive to physiological development.

Rapid increase in weight and height is possible.

Sudden crushes and hero worship.

Will question adult authority.

Wide range of maturity levels.

Boys more loyal to specific group than girls.

Interested in games involving teams.

Will tease opposite sex.

Interested in earning money.

May be inclined to be lazy and moody.

Concerned for appearance.

Desires privacy.

Needs someone to listen as problems are talked over.

Needs adult treatment to get good responses.

Thrives on growing independent.

Needs opportunity to verbally express thoughts and feelings.

Chapter Six

TRAINING PROGRAM

THE PROPOSED TRAINING PROGRAM was developed around five aspects of the visual perceptual process. These five areas are briefly described below. There are varying stages of performance in each of these areas as well as numerous ways in which an impairment to these abilities may be manifested. It is not, however, to be precluded that there are no other facets of visual perception. Research into other parameters is vitally needed.

Coordination of eye-motor movements is conceived to involve total body movement as well as eye-hand performance. It becomes necessary for the human organism to perceive visually in order to react motorically. Therefore, adequate coordination of eye-motor movements is an important part of both gross and fine motor functioning and, thusly, of educational skills such as writing, spelling, mathematics and the written tasks of language arts.

A second aspect of visual perception, for which programming is suggested, is that of distinguishing foreground from background. Involved in this process is the differentiation of an object, shape or form from its background. This skill is also a vital part of adequate visual perceptual performance and successful academic achievement.

A third general objective of the training program is the improvement of visual memory. Visual memory refers to retention of an image perceived through the medium of the eye. Acquisition of education is dependent upon acceptable visual memory.

Awareness of spatial position, another process programmed into the suggested training, involves the ability to recognize objects, shapes and/or other written symbols variously rotated in space, e.g. distinguishing a *b* from a *d*.

Academic success is dependent upon the individual's awareness of relationship to object, shape, etc., at a given point in space. The enhancement of this facility constitutes the fifth general objective of the training program.

There is considerable overlapping of objectives for the five aspects under consideration. For example, many of the activities recommended for training in the other four areas will also improve coordination of eye-motor movements.

Multiple objectives may have been developed for each activity; however, space did not permit inclusion of all of these objectives. It will be noted, also, that a change in the last objective is frequently made to show variation. For example, the final objective may have been changed from improvement of tactile ability to increasing kinesthetic sense while the procedures required actually were designed to improve both.

The program was developed to give general objectives and procedures for working with children with impaired visual perception. However, the trainer is to be aware, during implementation, that modification may be necessary to meet the individual need of the trainee. For example, the suggested verbalizations may be replaced by the child's spontaneous verbal response if the subject is capable of such performance.

GENERAL CONSIDERATIONS OF THE TRAINING PROGRAM

Some general considerations of the Training Program are as follows:

To involve the entire realm of sensory modalities.

To enhance techniques of motivation.

To avoid overarousal.

To provide for periods of relaxation and performance.

To choose child's most efficient performance period.

To repeat tasks presented the previous day.

To keep classroom teacher informed at all times of child's performance.

To correlate clinical training with classroom activities whenever it is possible to do so.

To increase language confidence of child.

To consider language environment of child in programming.

To utilize strength of performance to help child compensate for weaknesses.

To move from simple to complex, whole to parts, object to concept and concrete to abstract.

SPECIFIC GOALS OF THE TRAINING PROGRAM

More specific goals of the training program are outlined below.

I. To improve speech and language abilities.
   A. By including the language environment of the children and increasing awareness.
      1. Of body image.
      2. Of environment.
      3. Of kinesthetic sense.
      4. Of tactile sense.
      5. Of use of gesture in communication.
      6. Of objects, actions and speech in everyday experiences.
   B. By building up language confidence of children through improving specific skills.
      1. In visual attention.
      2. In auditory ability.

    3. In eye movement.

    4. In coordination of eye movement, gesture and speech.

    5. In spontaneous speech.

    6. In length of verbal output.

    7. In appropriateness of response.

    8. In recall and interpretation of spoken language.

    9. In rhythm speech patterns.

    10. In word-sequencing ability.

    11. In sentence recognition and comprehension.

    12. In articulation.

II. To improve academic performance.

    A. In reading and related areas.

    B. In number concept.

    C. In writing.

CONDITIONING PERIOD

Prior to presentation of the training program, it is advisable to involve subjects in a preliminary conditioning period. Some objectives of this conditioning period are (a) to promote a feeling of trust in clinician, (6) to improve ability to listen and (c) to improve ability to follow directions.

DAILY RECORD KEEPING

For daily record keeping purposes, the Daily Activities Check-off Lists (Tables V and VI in the Appendix) are recommended. These forms provide space for listing each activity presented to a subject and a place for comments about the subject's performance on a specific day. These may be altered to better serve the trainer's purpose.

FREQUENT EVALUATION

To provide continual, frequent evaluation during the training period, subjects may be rated every two weeks (see Individual Rating Sheets, Tables III and IV in the Appendix) .

Also, the tests described in Chapter 2, under "Measurement of Visual Perceptual Functioning," may be administered periodically to check the progress of the child.

In the case of a child with learning disabilities, it is recommended that all testing be done on an individual basis and at a time when the subject is at or near the peak of his performance. These times should be selected in consideration of the following:

    1. Is the subject on new medication?

    2. Has the medication been discontinued recently?

3. Does the subject perform better in the morning or in the afternoon?
4. Does the classroom teacher feel that this is a good day for the child?
5. Has the child been ill recently?

REWARD

The reader will note that throughout this handbook reference is made to emphasize programming to meet the needs of the child. With all children, it is important that they experience success in performance. This success, in itself, is a reward; however, it may be necessary to provide extrinsic rewards for performing to capacity.

PRESENTATION OF TRAINING PROGRAM

Following the preliminary conditioning, the training program may be presented. It is recommended that a minimal length of time for this training be thirty hours per child over a six-week period. Subjects may be removed from the classroom individually at times and in groups of three or four on other occasions. Most effective methods to be used with each child may be determined by trial and error. The daily period may range from thirty minutes to an hour, or longer, depending upon the child's attention span. Tasks may be presented indoors or outdoors, as the activity dictates.

PROGRAMMED TRAINING ACTIVITIES

Objectives	*Procedures*
I. To Improve Coordination of Eye-Motor Movements	
A. To improve visual-motor perceptual functioning by involving total body movement in gross motor activities.	
1. To enhance speech and language ability.	
a. To improve balance and body image.	a. Walk between two straight lines. *Verbalization:* "I'm walking from my house to your house."
	Walk between two curved lines. *Verbalization:* "I'm taking a walk."
	Walk between two lines in form of circle, square, etc. *Verbalization:* I'm walking around the moon." "I'm walking around the block.
	Use walking board. Walk forward; use arms for balance. *Verbalization:* "I'm walking forward on the board."
	Walk backward; use arms for balance. *Verbalization:* "I'm walking backward on the board."
	Walk to middle of board, turn, walk back. *Verbalization:* "I'm walking to the middle of the board."
(1) To create awareness of left and right.	(1) Walk forward to middle, turn, walk sideways, weight on balls of feet. *Verbalization:* "I'm walking to the middle." "I'm turning." "I'm walking to the left."
	Walk forward to middle, turn, walk sideward, right, weight on balls of feet. *Verbalization:* "I'm walking to the middle." "I'm turning." "I'm walking to the right."

Objectives	*Procedures*
I. To Improve Coordination of Eye-Motor Movements	
A. To improve visual-motor perceptual functioning by involving total body movement in gross motor activities.	
1. To enhance speech and language ability.	
a. To improve balance and body image.	
(1) To create awareness of left and right.	Walk forward with left foot in front of right foot. *Verbalization:* "My left foot is in front of my right foot."
(a) To increase awareness of prepositional speech.	(a) Walk forward with right foot in front of left. *Verbalization:* "My right foot is in front of my left foot."
	Walk backward with left foot in front of right foot. *Verbalization:* "My left foot is in front of my right foot."
	Walk backward with right foot in front of left. *Verbalization:* "My right foot is in front of my left foot."
(2) To create awareness of direction.	
(a) To increase awareness of prepositional speech.	(a) Walk forward, hands on hips. *Verbalization:* "My hands are on my hips." "I'm walking forward."
	Walk backward hands on hips. *Verbalization:* "My hands are on my hips." "I'm walking backward."
	Walk forward and pick up chalk eraser from board. *Verbalization:* "I'm walking forward on the board." "I'm picking up the eraser."

Objectives	*Procedures*
I. To Improve Coordination of Eye-Motor Movements	
A. To improve visual-motor perceptual functioning by involving total body movement in gross motor activities.	
1. To enhance speech and language ability.	
a. To improve balance and body image.	
(2) To create awareness of direction.	
(a) To increase awareness of prepositional speech.	Walk backward and pick up chalk eraser from board. *Verbalization:* "I'm walking backward on the board." "I'm picking up the eraser."
	Walk forward on board with eraser on top of head. *Verbalization:* "I'm walking forward with eraser on top of my head."
	Walk backward on board with eraser on top of head. *Verbalization:* "I'm walking backward with eraser on top of my head."
	Trainers hold wand twelve inches above board. Walk toward center of board. Step over wand. *Verbalization:* "I'm stepping over the wand."
	Walk backward toward center of board. Step over wand. *Verbalization:* "I'm stepping backward over wand."
	Trainers hold wand at height of five feet. Walk forward under wand. *Verbalization:* "I'm walking under the wand."

Objectives

Procedures

I. To Improve Coordination of Eye-Motor Movements
  A. To improve visual-motor perceptual functioning by involving total body movement in gross motor activities.
    1. To enhance speech and language ability.
      a. To improve balance and body image.
        (2) To create awareness of direction.
          (a) To increase awareness of prepositional speech.

Walk backward under the wand. *Verbalization:* "I'm walking backward under the wand."

Walk to center of board, kneel, rise, continue forward. *Verbalization:* "I'm kneeling on the board." "I'm standing up straight."

Walk backward to center of board, kneel, rise, continue backward. *Verbalization:* "I'm walking backward." "I'm kneeling on the board." "I'm standing up straight."

Walk backward, hands behind body. *Verbalization:* "My hands are behind me."

Walk forward, arms sideward, palms down, with erasers on hands. *Verbalization:* "I can hold the erasers on my hands."

Walk forward, arms sideward, palms up, with erasers on hands. *Verbalization:* "I'm walking backward." "I can hold the erasers on my hands."

Walk backward, arms sideward, palms down, with erasers on hands.

Objectives	*Procedures*
I. To Improve Coordination of Eye-Motor Movements	
A. To improve visual-motor perceptual functioning by involving total body movement in gross motor activities.	
1. To enhance speech and language ability.	
a. To improve balance and body image.	
(2) To create awareness of direction.	
(a) To increase awareness of prepositional speech.	*Verbalization:* "I'm walking backward." "I can hold the erasers on my hands."
	Walk backward, arms sideward, palms up, with erasers in hands. *Verbalization:* "I'm walking backward." "I can hold the erasers in my hands."
(3) To create awareness of direction and left and right.	
(a) To increase awareness of prepositional speech.	(a) Walk sideward to the right, weight on balls of feet. *Verbalization:* "I'm walking sideways to the right."
	Walk sideward to the left, weight on balls of feet. *Verbalization:* "I'm walking sideways to the left."
	Walk forward, kneel, straighten right leg forward until heel is on board and knee is straight. Rise and walk to end. *Verbalization:* "I am kneeling on the board." "I can put my right leg out straight."
	Walk forward, kneel, straighten left leg forward until heel is on board and knee is straight. Rise and walk to

Objectives | *Procedures*

I. To Improve Coordination of Eye-Motor Movements

  A. To improve visual-motor perceptual functioning by involving total body movement in gross motor activities.

    1. To enhance speech and language ability.

      a. To improve balance and body image.

        (3) To create awareness of direction and left and right.

          (a) To increase awareness of prepositional speech.

end. *Verbalization:* "I can put my left leg out straight." "I am kneeling on the board."

Walk backward, kneel, straighten right leg forward until heel is on board and knee is straight. Rise and walk to end. *Verbalization:* "I can put my right leg out straight." "I am kneeling on the board."

Walk backward, kneel, straighten left leg forward until heel is on board and knee is straight. Rise and walk to end. *Verbalization:* "I can put my left leg out straight." "I am kneeling on the board."

Continue as outlined in Newell C. Kephart's *Aids to Motoric and Perceptual Training* (1954).

        (4) To improve gross motor functioning.

(4) Roll on grass. *Verbalization:* "I'm rolling on the grass."

Run between two points. *Verbalization:* "I'm running."

Objectives	*Procedures*
I. To Improve Coordination of Eye-Motor Movements	
A. To improve visual-motor perceptual functioning by involving total body movement in gross motor activities.	
1. To enhance speech and language ability.	
a. To improve balance and body image.	
(3) To create awareness of direction and left and right.	
(a) To increase awareness of prepositional speech.	
(4) To improve gross motor functioning.	Hop on both feet. *Verbalization:* "Watch me hop."
	Kick large object. *Verbalization:* "Watch me kick."
	Throw large object. *Verbalization:* "I can throw."
	Climb (jungle gym). *Verbalization:* "I can climb."
	Skip. *Verbalization:* "See me skip."
	Step over real objects. *Verbalization:* "I'm stepping over the block."
	Step over imaginary objects. *Verbalization:* "I'm stepping over the toy."
(a) To improve body rhythm and awareness of left and right.	(a) March to music. *Verbalization:* "Left, right."
	Jack-in-the-Box. *Verbalization:* "Watch me jump out of my box."
	March through various patterns to music. *Verbalization:* "I am marching in a circle, through the number,

Objectives	*Procedures*
I. To Improve Coordination of Eye-Motor Movements	
A. To improve visual-motor perceptual functioning by involving total body movement in gross motor activities.	
1. To enhance speech and language ability.	
a. To improve balance and body image.	
(4) To improve gross motor functioning.	
(a) To improve body rhythm and awareness of left and right.	the letter," etc. March to counting. *Verbalization:* "I can count. 1, 2, 3, 4."
(5) To further improve eye-motor coordination.	(5) Present eye-hand coordination exercises as outlined in *Instructor's Guide, Pathway School Program/1* by G. N. Getman, O.D.
(6) To improve fine muscle coordination.	
(a) To further refine eye-motor coordination by use of concrete objects.	(a) Toss bean bag from one scoop to another. *Verbalization:* "I can toss the bean bag." "I can catch the bean bag." Move toy between two straight lines. *Verbalization:* "I'm moving the toy between the lines." Move toy between two curved lines. *Verbalization:* "I'm moving the toy between the lines." Move toy between two lines in form of circle, square, etc. *Verbalization:* "I'm moving the toy between the lines of the circle." Move toy on a straight line. *Verbalization:* "I'm moving the toy on the line."

Objectives	*Procedures*
I. To Improve Coordination of Eye-Motor Movements	
A. To improve visual-motor perceptual functioning by involving total body movement in gross motor activities.	
1. To enhance speech and language ability.	
a. To improve balance and body image.	
(6) To improve fine muscle coordination.	
(a) To further refine eye-motor coordination by use of concrete objects.	Move toy on a curved line. *Verbalization:* "I'm moving the toy on the curve."
	Move toy on the line of a circle, square, etc. *Verbalization:* "I'm moving the toy on the circle."
	Have child lie on back on large sheet of butcher paper. Draw around child. Cut out picture. *Verbalization:* "See me!"
1a. To improve concept of size.	1a. Sort large objects of various sizes. *Verbalization:* "This one is big." "This one is not so big."
1b. To sharpen tactile sense.	1b. Sort large objects of various textures. *Verbalization:* "I can feel smooth and rough."
	Use eye movement chart (see Training Kit). *Verbalization:* "I can count the dots." "I can feel the dots."
1c. To increase awareness of shapes.	1c. Sort large objects of various shapes. *Verbalization:* "I can find a circle."
	Draw geometric figures in the air. *Verbalization:* "I'm moving my arm in a circle."

Objectives	*Procedures*
I. To Improve Coordination of Eye-Motor Movements	
A. To improve visual-motor perceptual functioning by involving total body movement in gross motor activities.	
1. To enhance speech and language ability.	
a. To improve body image.	
(6) To improve fine muscle coordination.	
(a) To further refine eye-motor coordination by use of concrete objects.	
1c. To increase awareness of shapes.	Trace around large geometric figure, with finger, in sand. *Verbalization:* "I can feel a circle in the sand."
	Trace around large geometric shapes made of sandpaper, foam rubber, felt, cardboard, wood or plaster of paris with finger. *Verbalization:* "I can feel the shape of the circle."
B. To improve visual-motor perceptual functioning by including fine motor activities.	
1. To enhance speech and language ability.	
a. To improve body image.	
(1) To improve fine muscle coordination.	
(a) To further refine eye-motor coordination by use of concrete objects.	
1a. To increase awareness of shapes.	1a. Trace around geometric figures on blackboard with finger. *Verbalization:* "Here is a circle."

Objectives	*Procedures*
I. To Improve Coordination of Eye-Motor Movements	

B. To improve visual-motor perceptual functioning by including fine motor activities.

  1. To enhance speech and language ability.

    a. To improve body image.

      (1) To improve fine muscle coordination.

        (a) To further refine eye-motor coordination by use of concrete objects.

          1a. To increase awareness of shapes.

Trace around geometric figures on blackboard with chalk. *Verbalization:* "Now I see the circle."

Trace around geometric figures on paper with crayon. *Verbalization:* "I see my circle."

Trace around shapes with pencil. *Verbalization:* "I see the circle now."

Trace stencils of geometric figures made from various materials. Use chalk, crayon and pencil. *Verbalization:* "I can see the square."

Follow preceding steps, beginning with B, 1, a, (1), (a), 1a, first item, for numbers and letters. Use appropriate verbalization.

Objectives   *Procedures*

II. To Improve Ability to Distinguish
Foreground from Background

A. To improve visual-motor perceptual functioning by involving total body movement in gross motor
activities.

1. To enhance speech and language ability.

a. To improve balance and
body image.

(1) To increase awareness
of geometric forms.

a. Walk between two straight lines
upon which curved lines have been
superimposed. *Verbalization:* "I'm
walking between the straight lines."

Walk between two curved lines
upon which straight lines have been
superimposed. *Verbalization:* "I'm
walking between the curved lines."

(1) Walk between two lines in the form
of circles, squares, etc., upon which
straight lines have been superimposed. *Verbalization:* "I'm walking between the lines of the circle."

Walk on a straight line upon which
curved lines have been superimposed. *Verbalization:* "I'm walking a
straight line."

Walk on a curved line upon which
straight lines have been superimposed. *Verbalization:* "I'm walking on a
curved line."

Walk on the lines of a circle, square,
etc., upon which straight lines have
been superimposed. *Verbalization:*
"I'm walking in a circle, square,"
etc.

Walk on the lines of a specific figure,
e.g. the number two, upon which
other forms have been superimposed. *Verbalization:* "I am walking on
the number two."

Objectives	*Procedures*
II. To Improve Ability to Distinguish Foreground from Background	
A. To improve visual-motor perceptual functioning by involving total body movement in gross motor activities.	
1. To improve speech and language ability.	
a. To improve balance and body image.	
(1) To increase awareness of geometric forms.	March, hop, run, skip in all activities beginning with II, A, 1, a, (1), first item. Use appropriate verbalization.
(2) To sharpen awareness of shape of numbers and letters.	(2) Walk, march, run, hop, skip in all activities as outlined under II, A, 1, a, (1) using numbers and letters. Use appropriate verbalization.
(3) To increase awareness of various backgrounds; to create awareness of prepositions in speech.	(3) Have one child move another child from place to place with various backgrounds, e.g. tree, building, net. *Verbalization:* "I see you in front of the tree."
	Have child move large object from place to place with various backgrounds. *Verbalization:* "See the chair in front of the tree."
(a) To create awareness of size.	(a) Place one large building block in front of small blocks in a group. *Verbalization:* "See the little blocks behind the big blocks."
	Step over various sized objects placed on various backgrounds. *Verbalization:* "I am stepping over the ball on the grass." "I'm stepping over the little ball on the blacktop."

Objectives	*Procedures*
II. To Improve Ability to Distinguish Foreground from Background	
A. To improve visual-motor perceptual functioning by involving total body movement in gross motor activities.	
1. To enhance speech and language ability.	
a. To improve balance and body image.	
(3) To increase awareness of various backgrounds; to create awareness of prepositions in speech.	
(a) To create awareness of size.	Have child role-play and imagine that he is placing himself beside, behind, and in front of large trees, small trees, etc. *Verbalization:* "See me beside the big tree." "See me behind the little tree."
B. To improve visual-motor perceptual functioning by using concrete objects.	
1. To enhance speech and language ability.	
a. To create awareness of prepositions in speech.	
(1) To increase awareness of various backgrounds and foregrounds.	(1) Identify another child placed behind large-meshed fish net. *Verbalization:* "I see Bill."
	Identify another child placed behind small-meshed fish net. *Verbalization:* "I can find Bill."
	Identify toy, chair, etc., placed behind large-meshed fish net. *Verbalization:* "I can see the chair."

Objectives	*Procedures*
II. To Improve Ability to Distinguish Foreground from Background	
B. To improve visual-motor perceptual functioning by using concrete objects.	
1. To enhance speech and language ability.	
a. To create awareness of prepositions in speech.	
(1) To increase awareness of various backgrounds and foregrounds.	Identify toy, chair, etc., behind small-meshed fish net. *Verbalization:* "I can see the chair behind the net."
	Identify varied backgrounds behind an object. *Verbalization:* "I see the tree behind the chair."
	Identify backgrounds in large pictures. *Verbalization:* "The flowers are behind the girl."
	Identify object placed in front of frame upon which strings have been arranged vertically, horizontally or diagonally. *Verbalization:* "The car is in front of the lines."
	Identify object placed behind a frame upon which string, or yarn, has been arranged vertically, horizontally or diagonally. *Verbalization:* "I see the ball behind the lines."
(a) To increase awareness of shapes.	(a) Identify large blocks in shape of square, long box, triangle, etc., placed behind large-meshed fish net. *Verbalization:* "I can find the square behind the net."
	Identify large blocks in shape of square, long box, triangle, etc., placed behind small-meshed fish net. *Verbalization:* "I see the square behind the net."

Objectives	*Procedures*

II. To Improve Ability to Distinguish Foreground from Background

    B. To improve visual-motor perceptual functioning by using concrete objects.

        1. To enhance speech and language ability.

            a. To create awareness of prepositions in speech.

                (1) To increase awareness of various backgrounds and foregrounds.

                    (a) To increase awareness of shapes.

1a. To improve concept of size.	1a. Identify, by size, blocks placed behind large-meshed and small-meshed fish net. *Verbalization:* "The big block is behind the net."
2a. To sharpen awareness of color.	2a. Identify, by color, large blocks of various sizes placed behind large-meshed fish net. *Verbalization:* "I can see blue squares."
	Identify, by color, large blocks of various sizes placed behind small-meshed fish net. *Verbalization:* "I see the little squares behind the net. They are red."
3a. To sharpen awareness of color and number.	3a. Identify number of blue, yellow, etc., blocks of various sizes behind both large-meshed and small-meshed nets. *Verbalization:* "I see two big yellow triangles behind the net."
4a. To improve form constancy.	4a. Select like shapes (made of yarn) glued to inflated balloon. *Verbalization:* "See the circles on the balloon."

Objectives	*Procedures*
II. To Improve Ability to Distinguish Foreground from Background	
B. To improve visual-motor perceptual functioning by using concrete objects.	
1. To enhance speech and language ability.	
a. To create awareness of prepositions in speech.	
(1) To increase awareness of various backgrounds and foregrounds.	
(a) To increase awareness of shapes.	
5a. To improve concept of numbers.	5a. Count like shapes (made of yarn) glued to inflated balloon. *Verbalization:* "I can find three circles on the balloon."
(b) To sharpen awareness of shape, size, color and number.	(b) Place shapes to form framed puzzle. Identify according to shape, size, color and number. *Verbalization:* "I see two red circles in the puzzle."
	In dark room, identify objects to which luminous paint has been applied. *Verbalization:* "I see two trees." Identify according to shape, size and number. Use appropriate verbalization.
1a. To sharpen tactile sense; to create awareness of letters and numbers.	1a. Blindfold child. Identify raised letters glued to plywood, sandpaper, etc. *Verbalization:* "I feel the letter A."
	Blindfold child. Identify raised numbers glued to plywood, sandpaper, etc. *Verbalization:* "I feel the three on the sandpaper."
2a. To improve fine muscle coordination.	2a. Work puzzles of various designs, colors, backgrounds and composition. *Verbalization:* "See the tree

Objectives	*Procedures*

II. To Improve Ability to Distinguish Foreground from Background

  B. To improve visual-motor perceptual functioning by using concrete objects.

    1. To enhance speech and language ability.

      a. To create awareness of prepositions in speech.

        (1) To increase awareness of various backgrounds and foregrounds.

          (b) To sharpen awareness of shape, size, color and number.

          2a. To improve fine muscle coordination.

against the sky."

Move toy between two straight lines upon which curved lines have been superimposed. *Verbalization:* "The car is going between two straight lines."

Move object between two curved lines upon which straight lines have been superimposed. *Verbalization:* "The car is going between the curved lines."

Move toy between two lines in form of circles, squares, etc., upon which straight lines have been superimposed. *Verbalization:* "The car is making a circle."

Move toy on straight lines upon which curved lines have been superimposed. *Verbalization:* "The car is going on the straight line."

3a. To improve eye and hand coordination.

3a. Move object on lines of a circle, square, etc., upon which straight lines have been superimposed. *Ver-*

Objectives	*Procedures*

II. To Improve Ability to Distinguish Foreground from Background

  B. To improve visual-motor perceptual functioning by using concrete objects.

    1. To enhance speech and language ability.

      a. To create awareness of prepositions in speech.

        (1) To increase awareness of various backgrounds and foregrounds.

          (b) To sharpen awareness of shape, size, color and number.

            3a. To improve eye and hand coordination.

balization: "I am moving the car in a circle."

Move object on lines of a specific number, letter, word, etc., upon which other numbers, letters, etc., have been superimposed. *Verbalization:* "I can move the car on the number three."

Finger paint upon backgrounds of varied textures and colors. *Verbalization:* "See me cover up the sandpaper."

Trace around geometric figures with finger (in sand). *Verbalization:* "I can feel the circle in the sand."

Trace around geometric figure with finger (in clay). *Verbalization:* "I can make a circle in the clay."

Trace around geometric figures, made of sandpaper, foam rubber, felt, cardboard, wood, plastic or plaster of paris placed on varied backgrounds. Use finger. *Verbaliza-*

Objectives	*Procedures*

II. To Improve Ability to Distinguish Foreground from Background

B. To improve visual-motor perceptual functioning by using concrete objects.

    1. To enhance speech and language ability.

        a. To create awareness of prepositions in speech.

           (1) To increase awareness of various backgrounds and foregrounds.

                (b) To sharpen awareness of shape, size, color and number.

                    3a. To improve eye and hand coordination.

tion: "I can feel the shape of the circle."

Trace around geometric figures on blackboard with finger. *Verbalization:* "Here is a circle on the blackboard."

Trace around geometric figures on blackboard with chalk. *Verbalization:* "Now I can see the circle on the blackboard."

Use crayon to trace around geometric figures on paper of varied textures and colors. *Verbalization:* "See the circle on the smooth, red paper."

Use pencil to trace around geometric figures of varied textures and colors. *Verbalization:* "See the circle on the rough, red paper."

Trace around stencils with chalk, crayon and pencil on backgrounds of varied textures and colors. *Verbalization:* "I can make a circle on the rough paper."

Objectives	*Procedures*
II. To Improve Ability to Distinguish Foreground from Background	
B. To improve visual-motor perceptual functioning by using concrete objects.	
1. To enhance speech and language ability.	
a. To create awareness of prepositions in speech.	
(1) To increase awareness of various backgrounds and foregrounds.	
(b) To sharpen awareness of shape, size, color and number.	
3a. To improve eye and hand coordination.	Follow preceding steps, beginning at II, B, 1, a, (1), (b), 3a, fourth item, for numbers and letters. Encourage appropriate verbalization.

Objectives   *Procedures*

III. To Improve Visual Memory
  A. To improve visual-motor percep-
     tual functioning by involving
     total body movement in gross
     motor activities.
     1. To enhance speech and lan-
        guage ability.
        a. To improve awareness of   a. Have child move to all circles drawn
           geometric shapes.   on a patio. *Verbalization:* "I can find
                                              all the circles."

                                              Have child walk on lines of all cir-
                                              cles drawn on patio. *Verbalization:*
                                              "I am walking around the circles."

                                              Have child move to all squares
                                              drawn on patio, rectangles drawn on
                                              patio, etc. *Verbalization:* "I can find
                                              all squares, rectangles," etc.

                                              Have child walk on lines of all
                                              squares drawn on patio, rectangles
                                              drawn on patio, etc. *Verbalization:*
                                              "I am walking around the squares,
                                              rectangles," etc.

                                              Have child march, hop, skip and run
                                              on the lines of circles, squares, etc.,
                                              drawn on the patio. *Verbalization:*
                                              I can march on the lines of the cir-
                                              cles."

           (1) To improve awareness   (1) Have child move to like shapes of
               of color.   like color drawn on patio with color-
                                            ed chalk. *Verbalization:* "I can find
                                            all the blue circles."

           (2) To improve concept of   (2) Have child move to all small circles,
               size.   squares, rectangles, etc., drawn on
                                            patio. *Verbalization:* "I can find all
                                            the small circles."

                                            Have child move to all large circles,

Objectives	*Procedures*
III. To Improve Visual Memory	
A. To improve visual-motor perceptual functioning by involving total body movement in gross motor activities.	
1. To enhance speech and language ability.	
a. To improve awareness of geometric shapes.	
(2) To improve concept of size.	squares, rectangles, etc., drawn on patio. *Verbalization:* "I can find all the big circles."
(3) To relate concept of shapes to those within the environment.	(3) Have child identify and move to like shapes within the environment. *Verbalization:* "I see a circle in the wallpaper."
(4) To increase tactile sense.	(4) Have child move to, identify and touch like shapes within the environment. *Verbalization:* "I can see and feel the circle on the light."
B. To improve visual-motor perceptual functioning; to reinforce visual image retention by use of concrete objects.	
1. To enhance speech and language ability.	
a. To improve awareness of geometric shapes.	
(1) To improve awareness of likenesses and differences in shapes.	(1) Have child choose pairs of like sizes of shapes. *Verbalization:* "I can find two little circles."
	Have child choose pairs of like sizes of shapes from a group of graduated sizes of shapes. *Verbalization:* "I see the circles getting smaller and smaller."
	Have child identify like objects or

Objectives	*Procedures*

III. To Improve Visual Memory
   B. To improve visual-motor perceptual functioning; to reinforce visual image retention by use of concrete objects.
      1. To enhance speech and language ability.
         a. To improve awareness of geometric shapes.

(1) To improve awareness of likenesses and differences in shape.	shapes in the environment. *Verbalization:* "I see the round pillows."
	Have child identify like forms cut from various materials such as plywood, felt, sandpaper, cardboard, plaster of paris, rubber, etc. *Verbalization:* "I see the circles, squares," etc.
1a. To create awareness of color.	1a. Have child identify like shapes of like color in the environment. *Verbalization:* "I can find the blue circles."
	Have child identify like shapes of different colors in the environment. *Verbalization:* "I see the red (blue, green) circle."
	Have child identify all like shapes of like color of similar texture. *Verbalization:* "I see all red circles made of wood."
	Have child identify all like shapes of different colors and different textures. *Verbalization:* "I can find many circles."
2a. To develop concept of position in space.	2a. Have child identify shapes variously rotated in the environment. *Verbalization:* "I see the upside down triangle."

Objectives	*Procedures*
III. To Improve Visual Memory B. To improve visual-motor perceptual functioning; to reinforce visual image retention by use of concrete objects. 1. To enhance speech and language ability. a. To improve awareness of geometric shapes. (1) To improve awareness of likenesses and differences in shapes.	
3a. To increase size concept.	3a. Have child identify all small like shapes in the environment. *Verbalization:* "I see the small circles." Have child identify all large like shapes in the environment. *Verbalization:* "I can find all the big circles."
4a. To sharpen tactile awareness; to increase kinesthetic awareness.	4a. Have child identify and touch like shapes in the environment. *Verbalization:* "I can feel my hand going round and round."
5a. To sharpen tactile awareness.	5a. Have child identify and touch like shapes of similar texture. *Verbalization:* "I can feel the wooden circle." Blindfold child. Have child identify like shapes by touch. *Verbalization:* "I can feel the circles."
6a. To improve ability to identify shapes against varied backgrounds.	6a. Have child identify like shapes of similar size against varied backgrounds. *Verbalization:* "I see the circle on the table." Have child identify like shapes of different sizes against varied backgrounds. *Verbalization:* "I can find big and little circles on the table."

Objectives	*Procedures*
III. To Improve Visual Memory	

B. To improve visual-motor perceptual functioning; to reinforce visual image retention by use of concrete objects.

  1. To enhance speech and language ability.

    a. To improve awareness of geometric shapes.

      (1) To improve awareness of likenesses and differences in shapes.

7a. To improve color concept and figure ground discrimination.	7a. Have child identify like shapes of like color on varied backgrounds. *Verbalization:* "I can find the blue circles on the table."
	Have child identify like shapes of different colors on varied backgrounds. *Verbalization:* "I can find the red and blue circles on the table."
	Have child identify like shapes of like color and then group these. *Verbalization:* "I can stack the red circles."

C. To improve visual-motor perceptual functioning; to improve fine motor coordination.

  1. To enhance speech and language ability; to further reinforce visual image retention by use of concrete objects.

    a. To improve awareness of shapes.

(1) To improve awareness of likenesses and differences.	(1) Have child complete form board of geometric shapes. *Verbalization:* "I can place the circle on the circle."
	Have child complete picture puzzle

Objectives	*Procedures*

III. To Improve Visual Memory

   C. To improve visual-motor perceptual functioning; to improve fine motor coordination.

      1. To enhance speech and language ability; to further reinforce visual image retention by use of concrete objects.

        a. To improve awareness of shapes.

(1) To improve awareness of likenesses and differences.	of shapes. *Verbalization:* "This circle matches that circle."
	Have child match like numbers, letters, words, etc. *Verbalization:* "I can find all of the number fives."
1a. To improve sorting ability.	1a. Have child sort like shapes. *Verbalization:* "Here are all the circles."
	Have child sort like shapes of similar size. *Verbalization:* "Here are all the little circles."
	Have child sort like shapes of different sizes. *Verbalization:* "Here is a big circle."
2a. To improve sorting ability and color concept.	2a. Have child sort like shapes of similar color. *Verbalization:* "Here are all the red circles."
	Have child sort like shapes of different colors. *Verbalization:* "Here are red and blue circles."
3a. To improve sorting ability; to sharpen tactile sense.	3a. Have child sort like shapes of like textures. *Verbalization:* "I can find the cardboard circles."
	Have child sort like shapes of various textures. *Verbalization:* "I can find all the circles."

Objectives	*Procedures*

III. To Improve Visual Memory

    C. To improve visual-motor perceptual functioning; to improve fine motor coordination.

       1. To enhance speech and language ability; to further reinforce visual image retention by use of concrete objects.

          a. To improve awareness of shapes.

            (1) To improve awareness of likenesses and differences.

4a. To improve sorting ability; to promote reading readiness.

4a. Have child sort like pictures, numbers, letters, words, etc. *Verbalization:* "I can find all the number fives."

5a. To sharpen tactile and kinesthetic senses.

5a. Have child move toy between two lines in form of circle on varied backgrounds. *Verbalization:* "I am moving the toy between the lines of the circle."

Have child move toy on lines of all circles, squares, etc., with varied backgrounds. *Verbalization:* "I am moving the toy going round and round on all circles."

Have child make like figures as he finger paints. *Verbalization:* "I can make circles."

Have child trace various shapes in air with finger. *Verbalization:* I can make a circle."

Have child trace with finger (in sand) all like geometric shapes. *Verbalization:* "I can feel a circle in the sand."

Objectives	*Procedures*

III. To Improve Visual Memory

    C. To improve visual-motor perceptual functioning; to improve fine motor coordination.

        1. To enhance speech and language ability; to further reinforce visual image retention by use of concrete objects.

           a. To improve awareness of shapes.

               (1) To improve awareness of likenesses and differences.

5a. To sharpen tactile and kinesthetic senses.	Have child trace, with finger, all like geometric figures in clay. *Verbalization:* "I can make clay circles with my fingers."
	Have child trace with finger around like geometric figures made of sandpaper, foam rubber, felt, wood, cardboard, plastic, plaster of paris. *Verbalization:* "I can feel the shape of all the circles."
	Have child trace around all like geometric figures on blackboard with chalk. *Verbalization:* "I can see the circles on the blackboard."
	Have child trace around all like geometric figures on paper, using crayon. *Verbalization:* "I can see the circles on the paper."
6a. To sharpen tactile sense.	6a. Have child trace around all like geometric figures on paper, using pencil. *Verbalization:* "I see the circles on the paper."
	Have child trace around stencils of like shapes with chalk, crayon and

Objectives *Procedures*

III. To Improve Visual Memory

    C. To improve visual-motor perceptual functioning; to improve fine motor coordination.

        1. To enhance speech and language ability; to further reinforce visual image retention by use of concrete objects.

           a. To improve awareness of shapes.

              (1) To improve awareness of likenesses and differences.

                  6a. To sharpen tactile sense.

pencil. *Verbalization:* "I can trace circles."

Have child trace around like stencils with chalk, crayon and pencil on materials of various textures. *Verbalization:* "I can draw around the circles on the rough paper."

                  7a. To sharpen tactile sense and to increase color awareness.

7a. Have child trace around stencils of like shapes with chalk, crayon and pencil with backgrounds of various colors. *Verbalization:* "I can draw circles on the blue and green paper."

                  8a. To sharpen tactile sense and to increase awareness of symbols.

8a. Have child follow preceding steps, beginning with III, C, 1, a, (1), 5a, first item, using numbers, letters, words, phrases, etc.

Objectives   *Procedures*

IV. To Improve Awareness of Spatial
Position

  A. To improve visual-motor perceptual functioning by involving
total body movement in gross
motor activities.

    1. To enhance speech and lan-
guage ability.

      a. To improve awareness of
forms.

        (1) To increase awareness
of likenesses and dif-
ferences.

(1) Have child find and move to all rectangles drawn horizontally on the
patio. *Verbalization:* "These are all
alike."

Have child find and move to all rectangles drawn vertically on patio.
Verbalization: These are all alike.

Have child find and move to all triangles drawn base down on the patio. *Verbalization:* These are turned
alike."

Have child find and move to all triangles vertex down on the patio.
Verbalization: "These are turned
alike."

Have child find and move to all
diamonds drawn horizontally on
patio. *Verbalization:* "These are all
alike."

Have child find and move to all
diamonds drawn vertically on patio.
Verbalization: "These are turned
down."

Have child find and move to rectangles in like rotation on patio.
Verbalization: "These are all alike."

Have child find and move to tri-

Objectives   *Procedures*

IV. To Improve Awareness of Spatial
Position
  A. To improve visual-motor percep-
     tual functioning by involving
     total body movement in gross
     motor activities.
     1. To enhance speech and lan-
        guage ability.
        a. To improve awareness of
           forms.
           (1) To increase awareness
               of likenesses and dif-
               ferences.

angles in like rotation drawn on patio. *Verbalization:* "These are all
alike."

Have child find and move to diamonds, in like rotation, drawn on
patio. *Verbalization:* "These are all
alike."

Have child find and march, hop,
skip, run on lines of all rectangles
drawn horizontally on patio. *Verbalization:* "I can run on all of these
that are alike."

Have child find and march, hop,
skip, run on lines of all rectangles
drawn vertically on patio. *Verbalization:* "I can run on all of these that
are alike."

Have child find and march, hop,
skip, run on lines of triangles drawn
base down on patio. *Verbalization:*
"These are all alike."

Have child find and march, hop,
skip, run on lines of triangles drawn
vertex down on patio. *Verbalization:* "These are all alike."

Have child find and march, hop,
skip, run on lines of diamonds

Objectives	*Procedures*
IV. To Improve Awareness of Spatial Position	
A. To improve visual-motor perceptual functioning by involving total body movement in gross motor activities.	
1. To enhance speech and language ability.	
a. To improve awareness of forms.	
(1) To increase awareness of likenesses and differences.	drawn horizontally on patio. *Verbalization:* "These diamonds are all alike."
	Have child find and march, hop, skip, run on lines of diamonds drawn vertically on patio. *Verbalization:* "These are all alike."
	Have child follow preceding steps beginning with IV, A, 1, a, (1), first item, in identifying the shape that is in different position. Suggest appropriate verbalization.
1a. To improve awareness of self and peers in space.	1a. Have child duplicate process of lining up three children, facing the same way. *Verbalization:* "The kids are all facing this way."
	Have child line up three children with one facing a different direction. *Verbalization:* "This one is different."
	Have child place himself in same position as one child of three facing opposite direction. *Verbalization:* "I am like that one."
	Have child walk through a maze. *Verbalization:* "I can find the end of the path."

Objectives	*Procedures*

IV. To Improve Awareness of Spatial Position

  A. To improve visual-motor perceptual functioning by involving total body movement in gross motor activities.

    1. To enhance speech and language ability.

      a. To improve awareness of forms.

        (1) To increase awareness of likenesses and differences.

          1a. To improve awareness of self and peers in space.

Have child march, hop, skip, run through the maze. *Verbalization:* "I can find the end of the path."

Have child walk on line of arrows turned in various directions. *Verbalization:* "This one is turned to the left."

Have child march, hop, skip, run on arrows turned in various directions. *Verbalization:* "These are turned this way."

          2a. To insure left-right discrimination.

2a. Have child move himself to right of given line. *Verbalization:* "I am moving to the right."

Have child move himself to left of given line. *Verbalization:* "I am moving to the left."

Have child move another child to the right of the line. *Verbalization:* "I am moving John to the right of the line."

Have child move another child to left of a line. *Verbalization:* "I am putting John to the left."

Objectives	*Procedures*
IV. To Improve Awareness of Spatial Position	
A. To improve visual-motor perceptual functioning by involving total body movement in gross motor activities.	
1. To enhance speech and language ability.	
a. To improve awareness of forms.	
(1) To increase awareness of likenesses and differences.	
3a. To improve use of prepositions.	3a. Have child move himself and another child before, in front of, behind, beside a line. *Verbalization:* "I am in front of the line."
	Have child move various body parts to the left or right. *Verbalization:* "I can move my arm to the right."
	Have child move himself and another child before, in front of, behind, beside other objects. *Verbalization:* "I am in front of the house."
B. To improve visual-motor perceptual functioning; to reinforce concept of position in space by use of concrete objects.	
1. To enhance speech and language ability.	
a. To improve awareness of forms.	
(1) To increase awareness of likenesses and differences.	(1) Have child choose triangles in like position. *Verbalization:* "These are turned the same way."
1a. To sharpen tactile sense.	1a. Have child choose shapes of a variety of textures in like position. *Verbalization:* "These are turned the same way."

Objectives	*Procedures*
IV. To Improve Awareness of Spatial Position	

IV. To Improve Awareness of Spatial Position

B. To improve visual-motor perceptual functioning; to reinforce concept of position in space by use of concrete objects.

   1. To enhance speech and language ability.

     a. To improve awareness of forms.

      (1) To increase awareness of likenesses and differences.

Objectives	Procedures
2a. To improve color concept.	2a. Have child choose shapes of like color in like position. *Verbalization:* "These blue ones are alike."
	Have child choose shapes of different color in like position. *Verbalization:* "The blue, green and red are alike."
	Have child choose shapes of like color of like texture in like position. *Verbalization:* "These rough, red ones are all alike."
	Have child choose shapes of different colors and different textures in like position. *Verbalization:* "These are alike."
3a. To improve concept of size.	3a. Choose all small shapes in like position. *Verbalization:* "These little ones are turned the same."
	Have child choose all large shapes in like rotation. *Verbalization:* "All of these are large."
4a. To sharpen tactile sense.	4a. Have child choose and touch shapes in like position. *Verbalization:* "These soft ones are alike."

Objectives	*Procedures*
IV. To Improve Awareness of Spatial Position	
B. To improve visual-motor perceptual functioning; to reinforce concept of position in space by use of concrete objects.	
1. To enhance speech and language ability.	
a. To improve awareness of forms.	
(1) To increase awareness of likenesses and differences.	
4a. To sharpen tactile sense.	Have child touch shapes in like position of various textures. *Verbalization:* "All these are turned the same way."
	Have child choose and touch shapes of various textures in various textures in various positions. *Verbalization:* "These are the same shape but feel different."
5a. To improve figure-ground discrimination.	5a. Have child choose shapes on different backgrounds in like position. *Verbalzation:* "All of these are alike."
6a. To improve use of prepositions.	6a. Have child place shape in, on, under, etc., an object. *Verbalization:* "The ball is in the box."
7a. To increase awareness of right and left.	7a. Have child choose felt figure of left and right hand (or foot). *Verbalization:* "This is the right hand."
	Have child place felt figure of left and right hand (or foot) on flannel board. *Verbalization:* "This is the left hand."
	Have child place own right hand (or

Objectives	*Procedures*
IV. To Improve Awareness of Spatial Position	
B. To improve visual-motor perceptual functioning; to reinforce concept of position in space by use of concrete objects.	
1. To enhance speech and language ability.	
a. To improve awareness of forms.	
(1) To increase awareness of likenesses and differences.	
7a. To increase awareness of right and left.	foot) on right felt hand (or foot). *Verbalization:* "It's the same as mine."
	Have child choose all felt hands (or feet) like own right hand (or foot). *Verbalization:* "These are like mine."
	Have child choose all felt hands (or feet) different from own right hand (or foot). *Verbalization:* "These are different from mine."
C. To improve visual-motor perceptual functioning by use of fine muscle coordination activities.	
1. To enhance speech and language ability; to further reinforce concept of position in space by use of concrete objects.	
a. To improve awareness of forms.	
(1) To increase awareness of likenesses and differences.	(1) Have child reproduce in the air a shape in a specific position. *Verbalization:* "I made the upside-down triangle."

Objectives	*Procedures*

IV. To Improve Awareness of Spatial Position

    C. To improve visual-motor perceptual functioning by use of fine muscle coordination activities.

        1. To enhance speech and language ability; to further reinforce concept of position in space by use of concrete objects.

            a. To improve awareness of forms.

                (1) To increase awareness of likenesses and differences.

Have child place left shapes (of specific texture and position) on all like shapes. *Verbalization:* "These are all alike."

Have child use finger to trace around shapes (on paper) in same position as stimulus picture. *Verbalization:* "These look like that."

Have child use finger to trace around shapes (on paper) in position different from stimulus picture. *Verbalization:* "There are different."

Have child trace around shape (on paper) with crayon in same position as stimulus picture. *Verbalization:* "This is like that."

Have child trace around shape (on paper) with crayon in different position from stimulus picture. *Verbalization:* "This is different."

Have child use pencil to trace around shape (on paper) in same position as stimulus picture. *Verbalization:* "This is like that."

Have child use pencil to trace

Objectives	*Procedures*
IV. To Improve Awareness of Spatial Position	
C. To improve visual-motor perceptual functioning by use of fine muscle coordination activities.	
1. To enhance speech and language ability; to further reinforce concept of position in space by use of concrete objects.	
a. To improve awareness of forms.	
(1) To increase awareness of likenesses and differences.	around shape (on paper) in different position from stimulus picture. *Verbalization:* "This one is different."
	Have child follow above procedures starting with IV, C, 1, a, (1), first item, using letters, numbers, words, phases, etc. Use appropriate verbalization.
1a. To sharpen tactile and kinesthetic senses.	1a. Have child reproduce in clay, sand or finger paint a shape turned in a specific direction. *Verbalization:* "I made one lite that."
	Have child place felt shape on all shapes in like position. *Verbalization:* "These match."
	Have child choose felt shape in different position from given one. *Verbalization:* "This one is different."
2a. To augment concept of size.	2a. Have child place felt shape (of specific size and position) on all like shapes. *Verbalization:* "These are all alike."
3a. To improve concept of color.	3a. Have child place felt shape (of specific color and position) on all like

Objectives   *Procedures*

IV. To Improve Awareness of Spatial
Position
   C. To improve visual-motor percep-
      tual functioning by use of fine
      muscle coordination activities.
      1. To enhance speech and lan-
         guage ability; to further rein-
         force concept of position in
         space by use of concrete ob-
         jects.
         a. To improve awareness of
            forms.
            (1) To increase awareness   shapes. *Verbalization:* "These are
                of likenesses and dif-   alike."
                ferences.

Objectives	*Procedures*
V. To Improve Relationship to Space	
A. To improve visual-motor perceptual functioning by involving total body movement in gross motor activities.	
1. To enhance speech and lan-	
a. To improve awareness of forms.	
(1) To increase awareness of likenesses and differences.	(1) Have child place children to copy a circle, square, triangle, etc., of children. *Verbalization:* "This looks like yours."
	Have child place himself and other children to copy a circle, square, triangle, etc., of children. *Verbalization:* "We are like that circle."
1a. To strengthen concept of long and short.	1a. Have child place children to copy line of children. *Verbalization:* "My line is just as long."
	Have child place children to form a shorter line, and then a longer line, of children. *Verbalization:* "Mine is shorter (longer)."
	Have child place himself and other children to copy line of children. *Verbalization:* "We're just as long."
	Have child place himself and other children to form a shorter (or longer) line of children. *Verbalization:* "We are shorter (longer)."
2a. To improve concept of size.	2a. Have child place children to form a smaller circle, triangle, etc., than a given one. *Verbalization:* "Mine is smaller."
	Have child place children to form a larger circle, triangle, etc. than a given one. *Verbalization:* "Mine is

Objectives	*Procedures*
V. To Improve Relationship to Space	
A. To improve visual-motor perceptual functioning by involving total body movement in gross motor activities.	
1. To enhance speech and language ability.	
a. To improve awareness of forms.	
(1) To increase awareness of likenesses and differences.	
2a. To improve concept of size.	larger."
	Have child place himself and other children to form a smaller circle, square, etc., than a given one. *Verbalization:* "We are smaller."
	Have child place himself and other children to form a larger circle, square, triangle, etc., than a given one. *Verbalization:* "Ours is bigger."
3a. To improve awareness of direction.	3a. Have child place children to left or right of a given line of children. *Verbalization:* "They are on the left (right)."
	Have child place himself and other children to the left or right of a given line of children. *Verbalization:* "We are on the left."
	Have child place children to copy a line of children placed in various directions from a given point. *Verbalization:* "Mine faces the same way."
	Have child place himself and other children to copy a line of children placed in various directions from a given point. *Verbalization:* "We are

Objectives	*Procedures*

V. To Improve Relationship to Space

A. To improve visual-motor perceptual functioning by involving total body movement in gross motor activities.

1. To enhance speech and language ability.

a. To improve awareness of forms.

(1) To increase awareness of likenesses and differences.

3a. To improve awareness of direction.

alike.''

Have child place children on dots, drawn on patio, to copy a pattern of children. *Verbalization:* "These are alike."

Have child place himself and other children on dots, drawn on patio, to copy a pattern of children. *Verbalition:* "We are alike."

Have child walk, run, hop, skip, jump on lines of circles, squares, etc., drawn on patio. *Verbalization:* "I'm going round and round."

4a. To improve concept of near and far.

4a. Have child walk to various lines, at different distances, from a given point. *Verbalization:* "This line is near."

Objectives   *Procedures*

V. To Improve Relationship to Space
  B. To improve visual-motor percep-
    tual functioning by involving to-
    tal body movement in gross motor
    activities; to reinforce concept of
    relationship to space by use of
    concrete objects.
    1. To enhance speech and lan-
      guage ability.
      a. To improve awareness of
        forms.

        (1) To increase awareness   (1) Have child place objects (shapes) to
           of likenesses and differ-   copy circle, square, etc. *Verbaliza-*
           ences.   *tion:* "These are alike."

                                 Have child place shapes on dots
                                 drawn on patio to copy a given pat-
                               tern. *Verbalization:* "These are
                               alike."

        1a. To improve concept   1a. Have child place, on patio, round
           of long and short.   objects to copy a row of round ob-
                               jects. *Verbalization:* "Mine is like
                               that."

                                 Have child place, on patio, shapes to
                               form a shorter row of shapes than a
                               given one. *Verbalization:* "Mine is
                               shorter."

                               Have child place, on patio, shapes to
                               form a longer row than a given row
                               of shapes. *Verbalization:* "Mine is
                               longer."

        2a. To sharpen kines-   2a. Have child move object on lines of
           thetic sense.   circle, square, etc. drawn on patio.
                               Verbalization: "It's going round and
                               round."

        3a. To improve concept   3a. Have child place objects to form a
           of size.   smaller circle, square, etc., than a

Objectives	*Procedures*
V. To Improve Relationship to Space	
B. To improve visual-motor perceptual functioning by involving total body movement in gross motor activities; to reinforce concept of relationship to space by use of concrete objects.	
1. To enhance speech and language ability.	
a. To improve awareness of forms.	
(1) To increase awareness of likenesses and differences.	
3a. To improve concept of size.	given one. *Verbalization:* "Mine is smaller."
	Have child place objects to form a larger circle, square, etc., than a given one. *Verbalization:* "Mine is larger."
4a. To improve awareness of direction.	4a. Have child place object to left or right of a given line. *Verbalization:* "They are to the left."
	Have child place shapes to copy a line of shapes placed in various directions from a given point. *Verbalization:* "Mine is like that."
5a. To improve awareness of near and far.	5a. Have child move shape to lines drawn at various distances from a given point. *Verbalization:* "The circle is near the table."

Objectives	*Procedures*
V. To Improve Relationship to Space	

C. To improve visual-motor perceptual functioning; to improve fine motor coordination.

1. To enhance speech and language ability; to further reinforce concept of relationship to space by use of concrete objects.

    a. To improve awareness of forms.

        (1) To increase awareness of likenesses and differences.

        (1) Have child build tower of six blocks. *Verbalization:* "See how high it is."

Have child place forms in form in form boards. *Verbalization:* "This goes here."

Have child copy pattern on pegboard. *Verbalization:* "This is like that."

Have child match colored felt shapes. *Verbalization:* "These are alike."

Have child match puzzle parts to form whole figure. *Verbalization:* "See the boy."

Have child lace and sew punched cards. *Verbalization:* "It makes a circle."

    1a. To sharpen kinesthetic sense.

    1a. Have child reproduce, with finger, a figure in the air. *Verbalization:* I'm going round and round."

Have child reproduced a figure in clay, sand or finger paints. *Verbalization:* "I can go round and round."

Have child trace around object on blackboard with chalk. *Verbalization:* "I can go round and round."

Objectives	*Procedures*
V. To Improve Relationship to Space	
C. To improve visual-motor perceptual functioning; to improve fine motor coordination.	
1. To enhance speech and language ability; to further reinforce concept of relationship to space by use of concrete objects.	
a. To improve awareness of forms.	
(1) To increase awareness of likenesses and differences.	
1a. To sharpen kinesthetic sense.	Have child trace around figure on paper with finger. *Verbalization:* "See be go round and round."
	Have child trace around object on paper with crayon. *Verbalization:* "I can go round and round."
	Have child use stencils of various forms, on blackboard with chalk and on paper with pencil. *Verbalization:* "I can go round and round."
2a. To improve concept of size.	2a. Have child copy forms, made by connecting dots, of various sizes. *Verbalization:* "Mine is like that." "It is little."
3a. To improve color concept.	3a. Have child copy forms, made by connecting dots, with various colors of chalk on blackboard, and with crayon on paper. *Verbalization:* "These are red."
4a. To improve figure-ground discrimination.	4a. Have child copy forms, made by connecting dots, on various textures of materials. *Verbalization:* "See the circle on the rough paper."

Objectives	Procedures

V. To Improve Relationship to Space
  C. To improve visual-motor perceptual functioning; to improve fine motor coordination.
    1. To enhance speech and language ability; to further reinforce concept of relationship to space by use of concrete objects.
      b. To improve academic achievement.
	b. Have child use chalk, crayon, pencil in copying forms of letters and numbers. *Verbalization:* "See the letter."

THE TRAINING KIT

The Training Kit, described in Chapter 2, provides a variety of suggested aids which may be constructed by the trainer or purchased commercially.

The primary purpose in listing the items is to stimulate the trainer in developing innovative ideas. It is by no means a complete list. Any item may be altered and others added as the need of the individual child dictates. Flexibility of materials used is as important to the child's success as flexibility of programming.

A single item may be used in training to realize more than one objective for visual perceptual performance, e.g. balls of various sizes may be used for improvement of eye-motor coordination, visual memory and relationship to space. The Roman numerals in parentheses preceding each listing refer to a specific aspect of the outlined program, e.g. Roman numeral I refers to Coordination of Eye-Motor Movements, and specific use for the aid may be found in that section of the program. The word *All* refers to all five areas of the outline.

It will be noted that the articles listed serve to develop sensory-motor integration.

(V,I) Bean bag scoop. Two plastic detergent measuring scoops (cup size) and bean bag. One child tosses bean bag from scoop to another player.

(I, III,V) Balls of various sizes.

(I,V) Large plywood figure. Toss bean bag through various sizes of openings.

(I,V) Ring toss and horseshoe games.

(I,V) Balloons. For catching, batting, throwing, making papier-mâché.

(I,V) Pathway School Program #1, Eye-Hand Coordination Exercises by G. N. Getman, Teaching Resources, 100 Boylston Street, Boston, Massachusetts, 1968.

(I,V) Sequential Perceptual-Motor Exercises, Dubnoff School Program/1 Level 1, Teaching Systems and Resources Corporation, Teaching Resources Division, 100 Boylston Street, Boston, Massachusetts, 1967.

(I,V) Walking board (to be constructed).

(I,V) Balance board (to be constructed).

(I,V) Booklet. Aids to Motoric and Perceptual Training, State Department of Public Instruction, Angus B. Rothwell, State Superintendent, Madison, Wisconsin, 1964. Material developed by Newell C. Kephart.

(I,IV,V) Butcher paper. Have child lie down on butcher paper and have another child trace around body. Have child cut out figure and affix body parts. Cut two like patterns of fabric, staple together and stuff with paper for life-size figure.

(II,IV,V) Large paper dolls without facial features. Have child add body parts.

(I,II,IV,V) Large cloth doll with facial features which can be removed and then replaced. May be obtained from Ideal Toys.

(I,III,IV,V) Wooden puzzle, Changeable Charlie, with changeable facial features. May be obtained from Halsam Products Company, Chicago.

(II,III,IV,V) Large tagboard replicas of animals, birds, etc., cut apart in various ways. Have child reassemble.

(I,IV,V) Large tagboard card with punched outline of figure. Have child lace or sew to complete figure.

(I,IV,V) Various dolls and paper dolls for dressing and undressing. May have child manipulate extremities and use for placement in use of prepositions, e.g. under, on top of, etc.

(I, IV,V) Various sizes, shapes and colors of blocks.

(All) Board, Cellotex or plywood, in which cup hooks have been placed. To be used for matching, sequencing and visual association tasks. Duplicate sets of color chips, pictures, numbers, letters, etc., are available. Place one item on cup hook and have child place matching item over it.

(I,III) Large square of cardboard on which various geometric or incomplete shapes have been drawn. Have child place on them like shapes, made of felt, kept in envelope on back of cardboard.

(I,III) Duplicate set of tagboard chips with pictures, colors, words, numbers, etc., on them. To be used with item immediately above this one and for various games, such as Concentration and Old Maid.

(All) Various types of puzzles.

(IV,V) Set of family figures.

(I,IV) Pictures of familiar stories, e.g. "The Three Bears," to be used for sequencing of events and sentence completion.

(I,IV) Various pegboards.

(All) Form boards of various kinds.

(I,II) Plywood square on which upholstery tacks have been arranged in shape of geometric figure, number, letter, etc. Blindfold child and require that pattern be identified first and later reproduced.

(I,III) Feely box. Box, with obscured opening, that contains various items. Have child reach into box, feel item and identify it.

(I,III) Cardboard circle, divided into equal portions. Each portion contains numbers, words, pictures, etc. Like numbers, words or pictures are glued to clothespins. Child is to snap clothespins on matching picture.

(I,III) Large plywood board to which small felt circles have been glued in shape of a circle. This may be used for color concept, tactile experience and to permit observation of subject's ability to cross midline of body in using arm.

(I,V) Various stencils for tracing inside and around.

(I,III) Various shapes of various colors, arranged in pattern on tagboard.

Like shapes made of felt, or other materials, to be placed over pattern and then on flannel board in like pattern.

(I,V) Various sewing and lacing cards.

(III,IV,V) Patterns of hands and feet cut from styrofoam to be used for improving awareness of left and right.

(III,IV) Plastic table setting to be used for creating awareness of left and right.

(I,III,V) One-half egg carton. In bottom of each cup colors, numbers, letters, etc., can be drawn or pictures glued onto the bottom. Have child place duplicate in cup.

(I,IV) Play Tiles. Halsam Products Company, Chicago, Illinois.

(I,V) Yarn to be used in dot-to-dot activity preliminary to use of pencil.

(I,II) Hunting Trails, Perceptual Communication Skills, Developing Visual Awareness and Insight by Selma E. Herr, Ph.D., Instructional Materials and Equipment Distributors, 809 Kansas City Street, Rapid City, South Dakota, 1967.

(I,V) Jungle gym.

(II) Picture frame and yarn. Yarn to be put on diagonally, vertically, horizontally.

(All) Letters, numbers, geometric figures, etc., made in plaster of paris, sandpaper, clay, etc.

(All) Various ditto sheets which include activities for following lines, completing shapes, completing figures, following numbers to form a figure, Marianne Frostig Visual Perceptual Training Materials, matching copying patterns, showing likenesses and differences.

Miscellaneous: Overhead projector, tape recorder. Various noise makers to be used for auditory perceptual training in conditioning period.

BIBLIOGRAPHY

Abercrombie, M.L.: Visual perceptual and visuomotor impairment in physically handicapped children. *Percept Motor Skills, 18*:563-594; 1964.

Agranowitz, Aleen, and McKeown, Milfred: *Aphasia Handbook.* Springfield, Ill., Thomas, 1964, p. 7.

Anderson, James M., and Austin, Mary C.: In Buros, Oscar K. (Ed.): *Sixth Mental Measurements Yearbook.* Highland Park, N.J., Gryphon, 1965, pp. 855-856.

Ayres, A. Jean: Patterns of perceptual-motor dysfunction in children. *Percept Motor Skills, Monograph Supplement, 20*:335-368; 1965.

Ayres, A. Jean: *Perceptual-Motor Dysfunction in Children.* Monograph from the Greater Cincinnati District Ohio, Occupational Therapy Association Conference, Cincinnati, 1964.

Barsch, Ray H.: *Achieving Perceptual-Motor Efficiency.* Seattle, Special Child Publications, 1967.

Bartley, Howard S.: *Principles of Perception.* New York, Harper and Brothers, 1958.

Bartley, Samuel H.: *The Human Organism as a Person.* Philadelphia, Chilton, 1967.

Bateman, Barbara: Learning disabilities yesterday, today and tomorrow. *Exceptional Child, 31*:167-177; 1964.

Bateman, Barbara: *The Illinois Test of Psycholinguistic Abilities in Current Research. Summaries of Studies.* Urbana, U of Illinois Press, 1965.

Benyon, Sheila Doran: *Intensive Programming for Slow Learners.* Columbus, Ohio, Merrill, 1968.

Buros, Oscar K. (Ed.): *Sixth Mental Measurements Yearbook.* Highland Park, N.J., Gryphon, 1965.

Crawford, John E.: *Children with Subtle Perceptual-Motor Difficulties.* Pittsburgh, Stanwix House, 1966.

Cruickshank, William: *Psychology of Exceptional Children.* Englewood Cliffs, N.J., Prentice-Hall, 1963.

Cruickshank, William, et al.: *A Teaching Method for Brain-Injured and Hyperactive Children: A Demonstration Pilot Study.* Syracuse, Syracuse U Press, 1961.

Dember, William Norton: *Visual Perception: The Nineteenth Century.* New York, Wiley, 1964.

Eisenson, Jon: Perceptual disturbances in children with central nervous system disfunctions and implications for langauge development. *Brit J Disord Commun,* 21-32; 1964.

Frostig, Marianne: Teaching reading to children with perceptual disturbances. In Flower, Richard M., Gofman, Helen F., and Lawson, Lucie L. (Eds.): *Reading Disorders.* Philadelphia, Davis, 1965, pp. 113-1127.

Frostig, Marianne: Visual perception in the brain-injured child. *Amer J Orthopsychiat, 33*:665-671; 1963.

Frostig, Marianne, and Horne, David: *The Frostig Program for the Development of Visual Perception.* Chicago, Follett, 1964.

Frostig, Marianne, Lefever, D., and Whittlesey, J.: A developmental test of visual perception for evaluating normal and neurologically handicapped children. *Percept Motor Skills, 12*:383-394; 1961.

Frostig, Marianne, Lefever, D., and Whittlesey, J.: *Developmental Test of Visual Perception*. Palo Alto, Consulting Psychologists Press, 1964.

Frostig, Marianne, and Maslow, Phillis: Language training: A form of ability training. *J Learn Disabil, 1* (2) :105-114, 1968.

Gesell, Arnold, et al.: In Buros, Oscar K. (Ed.) : *Sixth Mental Measurements Yearbook*. Highland Park, N.J., Gryphon, 1965, pp. 807-809.

Gesell, Arnold L., and Ilg, Frances L., et al.: *The Child from Five to Ten*. New York and London, Harper, 1946.

Goodenough, Florence L.: In Buros, Oscar K. (Ed.) : *Sixth Mental Measurements Yearbook*. Highland Park, N.J., Gryphon, 1965, p. 727.

Goins, Jean Turner: *Visual Perceptual Abilities and Early Reading Success. Supplementary Education Monograph*, No. 87. U of Chicago, Chicago Press, 1958.

Johnson, Doris J., and Myklebust, Helmer R.: *Learning Disabilities*. New York and London, Grune, 1967.

Kephart, Newell C.: *Aids to Motor and Perceptual Training*. Madison, Wisconsin State Department of Public Instruction, 1964.

Kephart, Newell C.: Perceptual-motor aspects of learning disabilities. *Exceptional Child, 31:*201-206; 1964.

Kephart, Newell C.: *The Slow Learner in the Classroom*. Columbus, Ohio, Merrill, 1960.

Kirk, Samuel A., and McCarthy, James J.: The Illinois test of psycholinguistic abilities, an approach to differential diagnosis. *Amer J Ment Defic, 66:*399-412; 1961.

Kirk, Samuel A., and McCarthy, James J.: *The Illinois Test of Psycholinguistic Abilities*. Experimental edition, Institute for Research on Exceptional Children. Urbana, U of Illinois Press, 1961.

Knobloch, Hilda and Pasamanick, Benjamin: In Buros, Oscar K. (Ed.) : *Sixth Mental Measurements Yearbook*. Highland Park, N.J., Gryphon, 1965, p. 808.

Leibowitz, Herschel W.: *Visual Perception*. New York, Macmillan, 1965.

Lowder, R.B.: *Perceptual Ability and School Achievement*. Winter Haven, Fla., Winter Haven Lions Club, 1956.

McCarthy, James J., and Kirk, Samuel A.: *Examiner's Manual: Illinois Test of Psycholinguistic Abilities*. Experimental Edition. Urbana, U of Illinois Press, 1961.

Myklebust, Helmer R., and Johnson, Doris: Dyslexia in children. *Exceptional Child, 29:*14-25; 1962.

Olson, James L.: In Buros, Oscar K. (Ed.) : *Sixth Mental Measurements Yearbook*. Highland Park, Gryphon, N.J., 1965, p. 852.

Piaget, Jean: The cognitive theory of Jean Piaget. In Maier, Henry W.: *Three Theories of Child Development*. New York, Harper and Row, 1965, pp. 75-144.

Radler, D., and Kephart, Newell C.: *Success Through Play*. New York, Harper, 1960.

Roach, Eugene G., and Kephart, Newell C.: *The Purdue Perceptual Survey*. Columbus, Ohio, Merrill, 1966.

Schultz, Duane P.: *Sensory Restriction Effects on Behavior*. New York and London, Academic Press, 1965.

Siegel, Sidney: *Non-Parametric Statistics for the Behavioral Sciences*. New York, London and Toronto, McGraw, 1956, pp. 75-83.

Strauss, Alfred A., and Lehtinen, Laura E.: *Psychopathology and Education of the Brain-Injured Child*. New York, Grune, 1947.

Weintraub, Daniel J., and Walker, Edward L.: *Perception*. Bellmont, Brooks-Cole, 1966.

Wepman, J.: Dyslexia: Its relationship to language acquisition and concept formation.

In Money, J. (Ed.) : *Reading Disability: Progress and Research Needs in Dyslexia.* Baltimore, Johns Hopkins, 1962.

Werner, Emmy E.: In Buros, Oscar K. (Ed.) : *Sixth Mental Measurements Yearbook.* Highland Park, N.J., Gryphon, 1965, p. 808.

Werner, H., and Strauss, Alfred: Cause factors in low performance. *Amer J Ment Defic,* *45:*213, 1940.

Werner, H., and Strauss, Alfred: Pathology of figure-background relations in the child. *J Abnor Soc Psychol, 36:*236, 1941.

Wood, Nancy E.: *Delayed Speech and Language Development.* Englewood Cliffs, N.J., Prentice Hall, 1964.

APPENDIX

TABLE I
PERFORMANCE RATING SCALE

1. Excellent, consistent performance.
2. Excellent, inconsistent performance.
3. Good, consistent performance.
4. Good, inconsistent performance.
5. Fair performance.
6. Poor performance.
7. Unable to perform.

TABLE II

TEACHER RATING SCALE

Name of Child _____ Age _____

Teacher_____ School _____ Date _____

Please rate each item, using the rating scale in Table I, by placing an X in the appropriate square after the item.

Rating Scale

1. Poor coordination in large muscle activities

2. Poor coordination in fine muscle activities

3. Confusion in spelling and writing

4. Reading below grade level

5. Hyperactivity

6. Inconsistency of behavior

7. Inconsistency of performance

8. Perseverative behavior

9. Distractibility

10. Explosive and unpredictable behavior

11. Confusion in following directions

12. Demands excessive attention

13. Difficulty relating to peers

14. Poor logical reasoning

TABLE III

INDIVIDUAL RATING SHEET

Verbalization

with

Gross Motor Activity

NAME _____ TRAINER _____

DATE

	2nd Week	*4th Week*	*6th Week*
Output			
Intelligibility			
Complexity			
Length of Response			
Articulation Accuracy			
Appropriateness			

See Rating Scale in Table I

TABLE IV

INDIVIDUAL RATING SHEET

Eye-Motor Coordination

Motor-Perceptual Training

NAME _____ TRAINER _____

DATE

	2nd Week	*4th Week*	*6th Week*
Ability to skip			
Ability to hop			
Ability to walk on line of circle			

See Performance Rating Scale in Table I for scoring.

TABLE V

DAILY ACTIVITIES CHECK-OFF LIST

	M	*T*	*W*	*Th*	*F*	*Comments*
(May 15 to May 19, 19__)						

Eye-Motor Movements
Fine Muscle Activities

Trace Straight Line						
Verbalization						
Trace Curved Line						
Verbalization						

Performance Rating Scale 1, 2, 3, 4, 5, 6, 7. Highest rating is 1.

TABLE VI

DAILY ACTIVITIES CHECK-OFF LIST

(May 15 to May 19, 19___)

	M	T	W	Th	F	Comments
Eye-Motor Movements						
Total Body Activities						
Walk Straight Line						
Verbalization						
Walk Curved Line						
Verbalization						
Use of Concrete Objects						
Move Object on Straight Line						
Verbalization						
Move Object on Curved Line						
Verbalization						

Performance Rating Scale 1, 2, 3, 4, 5, 6, 7. Highest rating is 1.

INDEX